First published in Scotland in 2022 by Super Power Books
An imprint of the Super Power Agency

© Super Power Agency 2022

This book is sold subject to the condition that it shall not, by way of trade or otherwise, be lent, resold, hired out, or otherwise circulated in any form of binding or cover other than that which it is published. No part of this publication may be reproduced, stored in a retrieval system, or transmitted in any form (electronic, mechanical, photocopying, recording or otherwise) without the written consent of the Super Power Agency.

ISBN - 978-1-8382568-1-4


All letters in the book were written by the S2 pupils of Broughton High School and the volunteers of the Super Power Agency

Author photographs by Gerald Richards

Cover design by Jonathan Gould

Book design and layout by Alisa Lindsay
www.alisalindsay.myportfolio.com

Printed and bound in the UK by Inky Little Fingers
www.inkylittlefingers.co.uk

  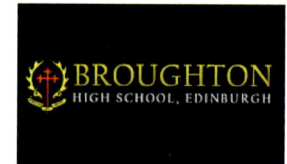

# CONTENTS

**FOREWORD** by Gerald Richards

**PAL PENS** - The Pen Pals of Mr Brown's Class

| | | | |
|---|---|---|---|
| Introduction | 1 | Dee & Martin | 65 |
| Aaron & Linsey | 3 | Emma & Claire S | 69 |
| Anja & Steph | 9 | Ethan & Elaine | 75 |
| Ayusma & Jan | 17 | Harrison & Claire H | 83 |
| Callum & Eileen | 25 | Josh & Francis | 91 |
| Cameron & Steph | 33 | Louisa & Catherine | 99 |
| Charlie & Siân | 41 | Ryan & Jo | 105 |
| Daniel & Will | 53 | Shefaly & Amerdeep | 113 |

**YOU'VE GOT MAIL** - The Pen Pals of Ms Anderson's Class

| | | | |
|---|---|---|---|
| Introduction | 123 | Maximillian & Sheila | 175 |
| Abigail & Valerie | 125 | Selina & Lauren | 181 |
| Adrianna & Maxine | 139 | Shaun & Liz | 191 |
| Angus & Alastair | 147 | Tor & Lucy | 199 |
| Ivan & Eduardo | 159 | Tristan & Charlotte | 207 |
| Leon & Adrian | 169 | | |

**ACKNOWLEDGEMENTS**

# FOREWORD

## ≽ GERALD RICHARDS ≼

We were entering into a new school year unlike any other in recent history. With COVID-19 restrictions in place in schools, the Super Power Agency had been unable to conduct our usual writing workshops with our school partners since April of 2019. We had to learn to adapt but how would we carry out programmes that rely on the one-on-one support our volunteer mentors provide to our young writers?

The magic of our work comes from the creativity that flows through every workshop AND the interaction of young people with our adult volunteers. For many youths, the only adults they deal with in their lives are parents, carers, and teachers. During our writing workshops, the pupils engage with adult mentors who are there to help support and guide them through their writing journey. Unfortunately, with COVID restrictions we couldn't bring the volunteers into schools and follow our normal routine. After speaking with our partner teachers at Broughton High School, a new pen pals project was born. This time all electronic, as the pupils and our adult volunteers corresponded via email (with the Super Power Agency acting as the go between, think electronic postmasters).

We asked the pupils to write a short biography of themselves as way of introduction for their new pen pal, and to help us match pen pals with similar interests. Our volunteers oversaw writing the first letter. After that, the correspondence flowed. For eight weeks these new pen pals wrote to each other about family, sports, food, fashion and sometimes COVID. New friendships were formed and as one young pen pal said, "I didn't know I could have so much in common with someone older than me."

We hope you enjoy these letters that give just a glimpse into the lives of people who came to learn that age is really only a number.

# PART ONE

# PAL PENS

## THE PEN PALS OF MR BROWN'S CLASS

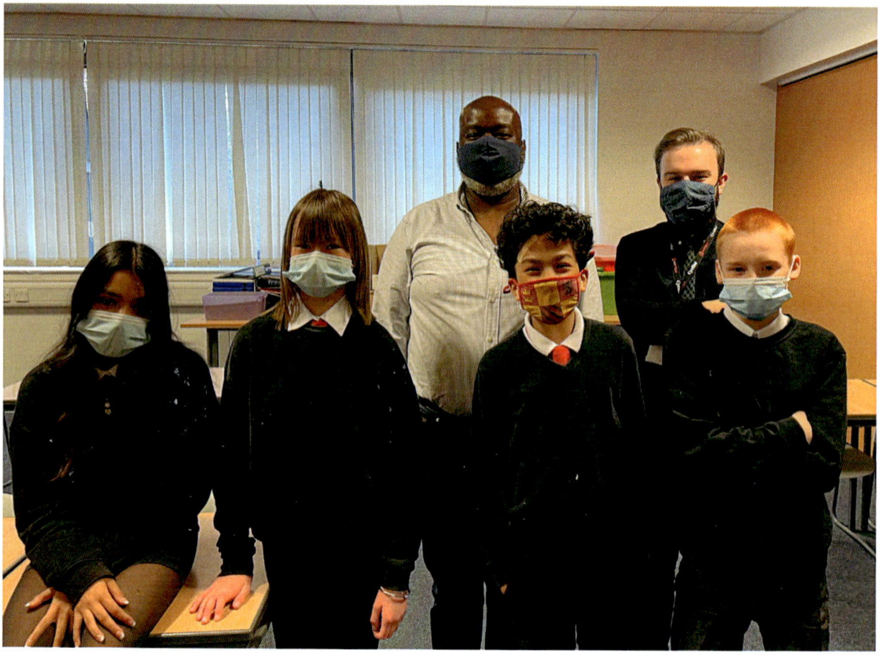

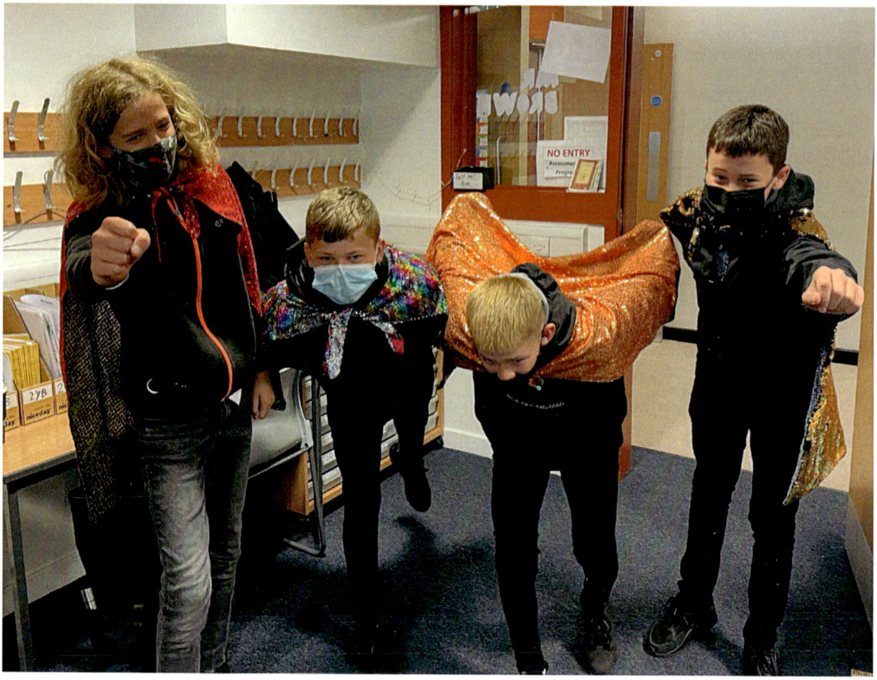
NO ENTRY
2YB
niceday

# Introduction

≽ AARON & HARRISON ≼

When Gerald and Jessica came into our classroom, we were nervous because they told us to write letters to people we didn't know, or 'randoms' as we called it.

**Aaron**: Some of us didn't want to write but when we got into it, it was fun.

**Harrison**: I was excited about it because it was surprising to see what people wrote about and what they were like.

But we both agreed, it was super fun. We were both very upset when it ended.

**Harrison**: We got to wear capes during the class!

**Aaron**: I missed that day!

If you have the chance to take part in a pen pals letter project, do it, because you never know what the experience will be. If you don't participate, you are missing out on good fun.

**Aaron**: And at the very end, you might get crisps like we did!

Thanks for reading!

From Aaron and Harrison in Mr Brown's class

# Aaron & Linsey

*Letter 1 - Aaron to Linsey*

Hi, my name is Aaron.

I like to play football, basketball and rugby.

When I grow up, I want to be a chef with my own restaurant. I like cooking, baking and gaming. Maybe as a pro I could travel and go to Germany.

I like growing plants. I like watching movies + TV. My favourite movie is *Star Wars*. My favourite TV show is *Brooklyn Nine-Nine*.

I love sweets.

I love ICT but my favourite subject is P.E.

Thanks for reading.

*Letter 2 - Linsey to Aaron*

Dear Aaron,

Thank you for your letter. Great to hear from you and to hear all about your hobbies. Sounds like you are busy with sport. Do you have a favourite? Are you part of any teams or do you just like the training part? I am a member of a gym where we do CrossFit which involves weightlifting, gymnastic movements, and bodyweight exercises. It's really fun (and hard work) and I've made some great friends there.

I also like to cycle and stand up paddleboarding in the sea – but not at the same time!

Being a chef would be an exciting career. Do you like to cook now? What is your favourite thing to eat? And what is your favourite thing to cook? There's a chef I really like just now called Yotam Ottolenghi, he is from Israel. His food is so full of flavour and colour. I bought one of his cook books recently, it's called *Simple*. I like the recipes as they are easy to follow and don't take much time. Although, there are some ingredients I've never heard of so that's fun to find those and try them for the first time.

You mentioned in your letter that you'd like to go to Germany. Is there something you would like to see or experience? I really like travel too; I think that's been one of the hardest things about the pandemic that we haven't been able to travel. But it does mean there has been more time for movies – I too like *Star Wars*. *A New Hope* is my all-time favourite movie. It was the first film I ever saw at the cinema. I still get goosebumps when I hear the music. Do you have a favourite *Star Wars* movie? Who or what is your favourite character? And what do you think of the new films that have been released recently?

I'm looking forward to hearing more about you, write back soon.

Best wishes

Linsey

P.S. I also love sweets; chocolate eclairs are my favourite but I like most sweets! What's your favourite?

*Letter 3 - Aaron to Linsey*

Dear Linsey,

I read your letter and I've got to say I like it, and I'm going to search up Yotam Ottolenghi.

You know, in primary I went to a cooking group and I met a Brazilian chef. I've been in newspapers for my soup-making, and I know how to make soda bread. My favourite sweet is a Yorkie. I love a Yorkie.

I would like to go see the Berlin Wall and the Anne Frank room.

My favourite movie is the new *Black Widow*.

From Aaron

P.S. I broke my thumb.

---

*Letter 4 - Linsey to Aaron*

Dear Aaron,

Great to hear from you. Thanks for spelling my name correctly. People often get it wrong as there are so many different ways to spell it!

How did you break your thumb? Does it have a cast or big bandage on it? Has it stopped you playing the sports you like? My son broke his arm playing touch rugby two years ago, it looked horribly painful.

I really like reading about all your successes with cooking, you must really enjoy it! I hope you kept a copy of the newspaper that you appeared in. Keep it up and keep exploring. What was the Brazilian chef's name? Do you remember what food he cooked?

I've not seen *Black Widow* yet, but I did go to the cinema last week for the first time since the pandemic started. We saw *Shang-Chi and the Legend of the Ten Rings*. It was great. Have you been to the cinema yet?

What did you see?

I have been to Germany but I haven't seen the Berlin Wall. My husband went with a school trip not long after the wall was broken down. He has a small piece of the wall with graffiti on it. I think Anne Frank's house is in Amsterdam, in Holland. I would add that to your list of places to go as it's a great place, with lovely people. Great food too!

I've been thinking about superpowers, and I wondered what superpowers you would like to have? I would like to be invisible and teleport.

Hope you've had a good week and your thumb doesn't hurt too much.

Speak soon,

Linsey

---

*Letter 5 - Aaron to Linsey*

Dear Linsey

I broke my thumb by jumping on the couch. I have a cast. I get if off on Monday. It did stop me from playing computer and sports. We're playing table tennis and I can play that cause I still have my good hand and I have been ping pong champion two weeks in a row, so I'm proud.

I don't have a copy of the newspaper and I can't remember his name but he taught us to make pasta and my superpower would be speed like Flash or Unkillable.

From Aaron

*Letter 6 - Linsey to Aaron*

Dear Aaron,

Can't believe this is our last letter! I'm glad you're getting the cast off your thumb, in fact you might have already had it removed by the time you read this. Good that you could keep playing ping pong and that you've been champion two weeks in a row – you're right to be proud of that achievement. That's brilliant, keep it up. You enjoy lots of different activities and hobbies – I think it's great to have a variety of interests. You must get to meet lots of different and interesting people.

Are you looking forward to the October holidays? I can't wait as I'm having some time off too. I'm going to Loch Tay with my family for a few days, which I'm looking forward to. The weather is looking rubbish but we will have lots of movies to watch and some board games too. I saw the new James Bond movie so I might need to watch all the earlier ones as I really enjoyed it. The rest of my family like the Marvel movies so we will probably watch some of those, including *Black Widow* – which I think you like too.

Will you keep writing after this project is finished? I like writing and use it a lot for my job which involves filling in application forms to ask companies and charitable trusts if they will donate money to other charities. I like to keep a journal too, writing down the things I've experienced or stuff I'm proud of. It's good to look back on and remember what you've achieved and things you've enjoyed doing.

Hope you have a great October break!

Best wishes,

Linsey

# Anja & Steph

*Letter 1 - Anja to Steph*

My name is Anja and I enjoy feeding the pigeons at my local park and listening to music and true crime stories. I have one sister who is two years younger than me. I argue with her for a living. I like shopping at charity shops and collecting crystals. My favourite food is chicken curry and Birds Eye fish fingers and many more.

I am half Scottish and half Finnish and can speak some Finnish. My favourite subjects at school are history, geography and English. I would like to visit the Scottish Highlands because of the views. I have a pet dog, she is a Staffie who is usually very hyper and likes licking people and doesn't like interacting with other dogs.

I don't really watch much TV but some of the shows I've enjoyed are *Death Note*, *Stranger Things* and *I Am Not Okay with This*.

*Letter 2 - Steph to Anja*

Anja,

This 'pen pal' thing is loads of fun!

As is working as a journalist. In my previous job writing for a daily newspaper in the US, I got to meet different people every day, tell interesting stories and learn all sorts of things. Similarly, writing for a tech website means following news about space and the latest gadgets.

For a time, I used to write about *Doctor Who* and other pop culture. Being a journalist is a real honour; it means connecting people with information.

I have lived up and down the east coast of America: Massachusetts to Florida to Maryland to Pennsylvania to New York! Have you ever visited the States? Is there anywhere in the US or abroad that you'd really love to see?

While I am fairly well-versed in the Zodiac Killer, I admittedly had never heard of the Hello Kitty case. Something new to learn about! Thanks for that recommendation.

I sell my linocut prints on Etsy. Have you ever tried reduction printing? It requires you to carve away material to leave only the pattern you want to print. It's great fun and a wonderful creative outlet. I am gearing up to start carving this year's Christmas Nessie and a Santa hat. I started the shop mostly out of curiosity; I wondered if anyone else would be interested in my art. And figured I might be able to make a little extra money to cover the cost of materials. It's been a wonderful journey so far.

I hope these letters aren't too long. The curse of a writer, I suppose. Looking forward to hearing more about you. Could you write your name out phonetically (spell it like you say it)? I want to be sure I'm pronouncing it correctly.

Until next time,

Steph

---

*Letter 3 - Anja to Steph*

Dear Steph

How has your week been so far? I also agree! Pen pals are great fun. Your job as a journalist sounds very interesting. If I had to visit one place/city in America it would probably be New York because of how pretty it looks at night. What was it like travelling up and down the East Coast of America?

I have never actually heard of reduction printing, but would love to learn more about it!

My name is actually pronounced like 'Anya' because my mother is Finnish and the 'j' in my name is pronounced like a 'y'.

Can't wait to hear more from you soon.

From Anja

Suggestion: I hope I've read everything correctly. If you don't mind, could you possibly type out your letter instead, if that's okay with you?

(Random would you rather question)

Would you rather drink mouldy milk for the rest of your life or would you rather watch your least favourite film over and over again forever?

---

*Letter 4 - Steph to Anja*

Anja,

As requested (and completely justified): a typed letter! I can barely read my own handwriting sometimes, so I don't blame you at all.

It's been a good week so far. Making progress on the house renovations, which is super exciting. I'm running the activities at tonight's Guide meeting, so I hope everyone has fun. How has your week been? Can you believe it's already the end of September?!

New York is absolutely amazing. If you think nights are beautiful, you should see the city during the winter holidays. Pure magic. Moving from state to state as a kid was actually pretty tough; I was always leaving my school and my friends and things that were familiar and comfortable. But, in hindsight, I think it was a great experience. I got to meet all sorts of different people from different backgrounds and experience new things that I wouldn't if I'd lived in the same town all my life. I for sure wouldn't have had the courage to move to Scotland on my own! I now wear that sort of nomadic life as a badge of honour.

Have you ever visited Finland to learn about your mum's heritage? My grandpa was from Poland, and I'd love to travel there one day to see where he grew up. It's so important to learn about our ancestors and carry on their traditions, stories, and memories.

This is my favourite time of year: autumn colours, cosy jumpers, cups of tea to warm my hands, and, of course, the return of *The Great British Bake Off* and *Strictly Come Dancing*! I started watching both when I moved to Scotland, and I even got my husband hooked on *Strictly* a couple of years ago. I love watching people dance and daydreaming about learning some moves myself.

Great would-you-rather question! I'd rather watch my least-favourite film over and over again forever. Which does sound like a bummer. But just thinking of drinking mouldy milk makes my stomach turn. Would you rather have to walk anywhere you ever go or have to listen to the Macarena every day?

Stay well and enjoy this beautiful weather!

Steph

---

*Letter 5 - Anja to Steph*

Steph,

Thank you for typing out your letter (I appreciate it).

My week has been good so far thanks. I've started a martial arts class and it's been really fun! I would love to visit New York one day with someone. I can't imagine how gorgeous it must be.

I've visited Finland multiple times with my family. We usually go during Christmas or summer to visit my grandparents who live in a small town in the south. During Christmas it snows a lot so we go skiing or sledging and during summer the temperature is usually around 30 so we go swimming every day.

Autumn is also my favourite time the year. My dad owns a house up in Aberdeenshire that was previously owned by my Grandma. We drive up there sometimes and stay there for a couple of days. I'm hoping to go there soon because of how pretty it looks in the fall.

My mother has also been watching *The Great British Bake Off* and *Strictly* too. I'm not as interested in them as I was before. In fact, I used to wear my mother's old skirts/dresses and dance around the room pretending I was on the big screen.

I would rather have to listen to the Macarena every day. I do like walking but I'd be too bored to do any of that.

Sadly this is my last letter ☹ but I hope we will get to meet at some point!

It's been nice talking. ❤❤❤

Anja

---

*Letter 6 - Steph to Anja*

Anja,

I'm gutted that this is my last letter to you. On the bright side, we'll soon get to meet in person (so I can pepper you with questions about where I should go if I visit Finland).

It sounds like an amazing place and is definitely on my countries-to-visit bucket list (which has obviously been put on hold, thanks to COVID).

My husband and I were supposed to travel to Mauritius in spring 2020 as a sort of very belated wedding celebration with his extended family who lives there. (We got married in September 2019). Alas, that was cancelled. I really hope to reschedule soon, though; I've heard such wonderful things about the country and am really keen to take a beach holiday. The sun and sand sound really nice right now, as I stare out the window at a gloomy, rainy, windy day. (I can smell my radiator heating up again for the first time since winter.)

I've been doing so much cross stitching lately that my hand is too sore and needs a break. Which is fine, because I want to start watching some scary movies to get into the Halloween spirit.

I particularly can't wait for November, when I get to celebrate Thanksgiving with lots of delicious food. It's my favourite holiday, with Chanukah (I'm Jewish!) coming in a close second.

Fingers crossed we'll be able to have a wee Christmas celebration in our still-under-construction house this year, ringing in the new year with a newly renovated home.

I hope we can meet soon. In the meantime, stay warm and healthy!

Steph

# Ayusma & Jan

*Letter 1 - Ayusma to Jan*

- Sport - running
- TV shows - *Outer Banks* it's so good
- Fav food - Curry brown lamb and white rice
- Fav subject - P.E. fun!
- Something about your family - They're brown Nepali and fun
- Have a sister and brother
- Fun thing to do - buying stuff
- Food don't like - pizza and cakes
- Fav place - Nepal so many places to see, the weather is hot.

*Letter 2 - Jan to Ayusma*

Hi Ayusma,

My name is Jan and I live in Edinburgh. I was born near Glasgow and lived in London for many years. I've also lived a little bit in France and Italy as I studied French and Italian at university. Languages were my favourite subjects at school. Do you speak Nepali? It's so cool to be able to speak more than one language. Have you always lived in Edinburgh or were you born in Nepal? It must be brilliant to be able to visit, although I guess it's a long way! When did you last go there?

I noticed we have a hobby in common – running! I love running. I didn't start doing it until I was a grown-up (nearly 30 years old!), but now I run a lot and during the last lockdown I ran every day to keep my body moving. I have run four marathons and lots of half marathons over the years. I ran a half marathon last week. It was really hilly! Do you like running outside? Do you like running on a track like the athletes at the Olympics? Did you watch the Olympics this year? I loved it and watched the highlights most nights. I really liked finding out about sports I didn't know much about.

I was wondering what you enjoyed doing in PE? Do you like team sports?

In my family, I'm married and I have two children – a boy of 14 and a girl who has just turned 11. Like you, I have a brother and a sister. I'm in the middle – my brother is younger and my sister older. How about you?

As well as running, I really enjoy reading and going to the cinema. I play netball too, although I haven't been able to do that recently because of an injury. I also like baking and making jam, which is really easy – just fruit and lots of sugar! I see your favourite food is lamb curry and rice. Do you like cooking? Do you sometimes do that at home?

Last year I learned how to do bookbinding, which is making little books, so I try and do that too when I have time. It fits in quite well with what I do, as I make books in my job. I'm an editor and translator and I work on making bilingual dictionaries – you might have some of them in your classroom or school library.

Are you enjoying being back at school? How did you find doing schoolwork in lockdown? I'll bet it was tricky and not so much fun without your friends around.

I'm looking forward to hearing more from you, Ayusma.

Jan x

*Letter 3 - Ayusma to Jan*

Hi Jan,

Oh, I just read your letter how long did you live in France and Italy? Yes, I do speak Nepali and I wasn't born in Nepal and I have only lived in Edinburgh but I do visit Nepal in the Summer but couldn't sadly go this year because of COVID. Have you ever gone anywhere else other than France or Italy?

I used to play every running game in Primary, and yes I love running outside. I love to race. I love winning but hate losing. I love P.E., my favourite subject. I love team sports. It is always so much fun!

I have a younger sister and an older brother who is 17 years old and a sister who just turned seven years old. Her birthday is the 2nd of September and so I am a middle child too!

I am enjoying school to be honest. I thought I wouldn't be up for it but I mean yes and no. I found the Wi-Fi quite annoying during lockdown and it was hard for me not to see my friends. How did you find it? And did you always want to make books?

Aysuma

*Letter 4 - Jan to Ayusma*

Hi Ayusma,

I was really happy to receive your letter. Thanks for writing to me.

I'm so impressed that you speak Nepali. Is it very different to English? I imagine it must be. And are you able to write it too? The script looks so beautiful—like art more than words. I'm sorry you haven't been able to visit Nepal for a while. Hopefully next Summer? Do you have family living there? Aunts, cousins, grandparents? They must miss seeing you and your family.

I used to do a job that involved quite a lot of travelling as I was making dictionaries in different languages. When I was working on Portuguese dictionaries, I visited Brazil quite often—that was definitely my favourite. The people were so friendly and helpful. I was mostly in São Paulo, but I did also visit the south of the country and another time I did a short trip to the rain forest.

Are you able to play in any team sports at school or outside of school? Football or netball maybe? Do any of your friends like running? It sounds like you'd be very good at competing in races—very determined!

Your sister shares a birthday with my daughter! Funny that we're both middle children. I think we're the ones in the family that are good at doing things—not the pressure of being the eldest and not the baby either. We just get on with things. What do you think?!

I'm glad you're happy to be back at school. I think it must have been so hard for young people to not see their friends and have to work online all the time. Especially if everyone else in the house is trying to work or be online too. Let's hope we don't go back to that... I found lockdown quite hard too. It was so intense just being with my family all of the time. I really missed my friends too. I often run with three other women, so we would film little videos or silly photos of ourselves when we went out for a run and share with the others. I didn't really like Zoom or video calls. I was much happier when I could see people again.

I'm not sure that I always wanted to make books, but I do think that I always wanted to work with foreign languages. I remember when I was about 10 reading a book about a girl who went to work in Paris, and I decided that I wanted to do something like that. It's a fun job that I do and I really enjoy it when I see the books in shops or on bookshelves. Funny to think about the words on my computer making it onto pages and into books. Do you have any idea of what you might like to do when you're older?

Looking forward to hearing from you soon. Take care.

Jan x

*Letter 5 - Ayusma to Jan*

Dear Jan,

Yes, it is quite different from English. I used to take Nepali classes but it was hard and I wasn't really good at it. I am looking forward to going to Nepal. I have almost all my family in Nepal.

Wow, I love your old job! Do you ever miss it?

No, sadly I don't. Some of my friends like walking, and they call me a fast walker.

Ha ha that's so funny! I am very determined when someone wants to race. Probs we are the ones that are really good at things, yeah, I get what you mean.

I want to be a detective in the FBI 'cause ever since I was a young girl I wanted to be that, and catch bad guys and solve things, and just help people.

Aysuma x

---

*Letter 6 - Jan to Ayusma*

Hi Ayusma,

I think this is my last letter to you. I've really enjoyed reading your letters to me.

It feels like autumn is on the way. I think it's my favourite season – I really love it when the leaves change colours and start to fall. Do you ever go to the Botanics? It's so beautiful there in autumn in particular, I think.

You asked me if I missed my old job. Sometimes I do, especially the travelling, but actually I'm thinking about doing something different for a job now. I'm going to do a course to become a software developer.

I think it will be quite a challenge! I'm looking forward to learning something new and I hope I'll still be able to use my languages if possible.

I can imagine classes in Nepali must have been really difficult. Maybe it's something you can come back to when you're older. For now though, it's very cool that you can speak it. You should feel very proud.

I like your idea of joining the FBI! It sounds like something you've always wanted to do and solving things and helping people is a brilliant thing to aim for.

Maybe we'll get to meet in person one day. I hope so. Until then, good luck and have fun!

Jan x

---

*Letter 7 - Ayusma to Jan*

Dear Jan,

I really liked writing to you. My favourite season is winter. I love the snow. Never went to Botanics. Which languages do you wanna learn?

I hope I meet you soon. You really seem like a cool person and fun. And I hope you do well as a software developer.

Aysuma

(Thank you for writing to me.)

*Letter 8 - Jan to Ayusma*

Hi Ayusma,

I thought my last letter was to be the last one, but I was wrong, so here I am again!

Hope you've had a good week. I've mostly been trying to avoid getting caught in showers and as I type this, it is POURING down outside! I've been doing quite a lot of running this week and have been soaked a few times…

I've been enjoying watching quite a lot of TV this week. I love *Bake Off* and I've been watching *Strictly* with my daughter. Do you like those programmes? I also really like a TV programme called *Ghosts* and I've been binge watching all the episodes on iPlayer.

On Saturday I went to see the new Marvel movie with my daughter and her friend. She got a voucher for Vue for her birthday and was really keen to spend it. I didn't think I'd enjoy it, but actually I loved it! It's called *Shang-Chi and the Legend of the Ten Rings*. He's the first Asian Marvel superhero. It was so good and the first time I'd been at the cinema in ages. Do you like the Marvel movies?

My niece, who is 19, is a student at Edinburgh University. She's in second year and is studying Spanish, so she's now back living in Edinburgh. We're really enjoying seeing her now she's here and she often comes round for dinner. She has a sort of 'pen pal' herself. It's a girl who lives in Spain and last year during lockdown they met once a week on Zoom. The Spanish girl is studying English and my niece is studying Spanish, so they each speak to each other in the other person's language so they can practise. It's a really cool idea and they've become great friends. Do you ever speak to your family or friends in Nepal on Zoom?

Is school going ok? Does it feel quite normal now? It's the holidays soon, so I hope you enjoy the break.

Jan x

# Callum & Eileen

*Letter 1 - Callum to Eileen*

I like to do mountain biking in my free time because it keeps you fit and I love being outside all the time. I like doing all the big jumps but the pump rock is my favourite.

I play football. I play for Hibernian football club. I have played for them for the seventh year now but I have played for other teams like Celtic, St Mirren, Hearts, Falkirk and Rangers.

The only TV shows I like are *Formula 1 Drive to Survive* or *Sunderland Till I Die*, they're just a bit different.

My favourite food is Bolognese because it gives you energy for training and games and the pasta is really nice.

My favourite subject in school is PE because I'm always active.

*Letter 2 - Eileen to Callum*

Dear Callum,

Thank you very much for your letter; it was great to receive it and to learn of your interests. I get the impression that you keep very busy and enjoy lots of sports, either taking part or watching on TV.

Your writing is much clearer than mine so I thought I would type this so that, at least, for the first letter exchange, you do not have to spend ages trying to read my handwriting.

I learned lots from your letter. I checked out *Sunderland Till I Die* – looks awesome even though I am not a huge football fan. What position do you play – probably not goal-keeper – I imagine you running about?

Mountain biking sounds and looks very exciting. I wonder what it felt like the first time you did one of the big jumps?

I cycle sometimes but mostly walk a lot, most days; my trainers don't seem to last that long! There are woods near where I live and just now there are lots of fungus/fungi; unfortunately I don't know enough about them to know which ones are safe to eat, so I just leave them alone. I am hoping there will be plenty of brambles for me to pick too in the woods and then I can make bramble and apple crumble.

I share your liking for pasta; it is one of my favourite foods. I like Bolognese too. I don't eat meat so make it with Quorn. I also eat fish, so I am not a proper vegetarian.

What other foods do you like? What would be your favourite meal? Who would you invite to share it with you? You can only have one footballer and one Formula 1 driver.

I hope I haven't asked you too many questions – you don't have to answer them all!

I hope you have a good week and look forward to hearing from you.

Regards

Eileen

---

*Letter 3 - Callum to Eileen*

Dear Eileen,

I have just read the letter you sent me, I am very thankful that you have spent time doing that for me. I get the impression that you are very active and adventurous.

I don't support Sunderland but have got very attached to it because some bits are sad then they have some good bits. I support Hibs in Scotland and Manchester United in England. I'm 12, what about you?

I love mountain biking. The first big jump I did I felt so good. All my friends came over to me cheering and hugged me. I jumped off my bike and threw it. Do you love cycles or just short ones?

I play football a lot, that's my preferred thing to do at my club. I train three to four times a week and I play one game on the weekend. I play for my boyhood club Hibs, this is my seventh year there but I have been to other teams like St Mirren, Rangers and Celtic. I get new boots a lot even if I don't need them. Just now I have seven pairs that fit me just now over £150 each.

I have Bolognese twice a week before training to get energy before it. I like BBQ pork as well. If I had to eat it with a footballer it would be Ronaldo because he is so hard working as a footballer.

Sorry I couldn't answer everything I didn't have enough time.

Regards,

Callum

---

*Letter 4 - Eileen to Callum*

Dear Callum,

Thank you very much for your letter; it was great to hear your news. I was very taken with your description of your mountain biking which certainly sounds very exciting.

I am a much more modest cyclist—where I live is quite hilly so getting going takes me a bit of effort and the surrounding countryside is also hilly. My cycle trips vary from a couple of miles to around 14–20. I was walking at the weekend, getting wet on Sunday afternoon and then things brightened up and it was lovely and clear with views for miles. I usually walk three to four miles each day, with a longer walk at weekends.

I did manage to pick some brambles when out walking. I also lifted the last of our potatoes and picked our pears—all four of them—an improvement on last year when there were only three!! The potatoes were disappointing, not that tasty and so will have to get a better variety next year.

I recall your saying PE is your favourite lesson at school. What is your least favourite? Maths was my least favourite and English my favourite. I liked PE too though, especially cross-country running.

My love of reading came from my school days and I really enjoy escaping into books. I have a soft spot for crime novels, nothing gory though. I use a Kindle sometimes but I prefer actual books where I can really turn the pages. Do you have any favourite books? I realise your football training might mean you are too busy?

I have two great nephews, the younger one just started school this year and will be five very soon. I have sent him a stripey hoodie top for his birthday. I also bought him a book of jokes for five year olds—I found lots of them funny so I hope they make him laugh too—or at least smile.

I hope you have had a good week and that this finds all going well for you.

Regards

Eileen

*Letter 5 - Callum to Eileen*

Hello Eileen,

- Thank you for writing back to me and for answering my questions. I was taken away with the amount you wrote back to me.
- I was surprised at the number of miles you cycle and walk at the weekends.
- I'm glad you got the four pears, but not so sure about the potatoes!
- I like maths. I have lots of my friends in my class and I'm good at it. I'm not good at English, but it's fun.
- I don't like reading, I never have, but I don't have time, like you said. But is there anything you would recommend for me to read?
- I have three sisters and one brother - we're a very big family.
- Would you rather get chased by five mini cheetahs or one big lion?

I hope you have a great week and everything goes well for you, and that you're still cycling and walking.

Regards

Callum

*Letter 6 - Eileen to Callum*

Dear Callum,

Thank you very much again for your letter and all your news, which I enjoyed.

I am glad to hear you enjoy maths and are good at it; it is a really important subject, so well done you.

I hope also that your pasta-fuelled training continues to go well too. I am still walking most days, but not cycling so much. Recent walks in the woods have been very lovely with sightings of deer; quite young ones on the path just ahead. I am not sure if they pick up on the sound, sight or smell first as humans approach but they are quick to scamper away.

I am wondering if you could choose to be any animal what would you choose to be? I liked your question about being chased by five mini cheetahs or one big lion. Cheetahs are so fast, and with five of them, even if one of them got tired, there would be others to take over, so perhaps being chased by one lion would be slightly better. I am wondering if I might land lucky and the lion might be vegetarian and not want to eat me after all. What do you think?

I see from your letter that you have three sisters and a brother. I have one sister and when I was little, although she is younger than me, she was definitely in charge. Are you the youngest or in the middle?

I will have a think about books given you asked if I have any recommendations. I am learning French and have been reading a book in French, but don't worry I won't recommend that one.

I hope that you have a good week and I look forward to your next letter.

Best wishes

Eileen

---

*Letter 7 - Callum to Eileen*

Dear Eileen,

I enjoyed reading your letter once again.

I am glad to hear you are still walking. I was surprised that you saw a deer on your walk. I didn't know they were scared of humans though.

Pasta is still fuelling me up for training.

If I were to choose one animal to be I would probably be a panda because no one attacks them, they're so chilled and cool.

I am going to Portugal on the 15th. It was nice getting to know you. If we get to meet you, I'll see you then.

Regards

Callum

---

*Letter 8 - Eileen to Callum*

Dear Callum,

Thank you very much for your newsy letter.

I realise this is my last time of writing to you and so I have inflicted my handwriting on you! I thought you might like this Puffin card: a few weeks ago I was in Shieldaig and bought several cards from Lisa Fenton who has a studio there. I hope you have a super holiday in Portugal. How exciting to be able to go on a flight and to enjoy a different culture and climate. Have fun.

I have enjoyed our letter exchanges and hope you have too. I will watch for a Callum B in football teams in the future. I wish you every success in whatever you choose to do.

Best wishes

Eileen

For: Cameron N                                From: Steph P

Hi Cameron,
Firstly Thanks for your letter!
It sounds like you are really good at football, do you love playing for a team? I have to admit that I don't know much, is the centreback someone who helps defend? Do you count goals stopped in the same way as goals scored? Is it a position you like?
I have a son who plays football but he is only six - his games are very exciting and the parents are very enthusiastic but most of the goals are scored by chance! There is one kid who often just sits on the floor in front of the goal!
What makes Liverpool so good? I have been once but not to the football - would you like to play for them?
I like some sports too - running and swimming and anything outside but I don't do any team sports. Could you reccomend something for beginners?
That sounds like a really long way to travel for school, do you mind? I live in Edinburgh too and go to university in Stirling so also have a long way to get there but I don't mind too much as I like listening to music while I drive (or sometimes lectures or homework if I've run out of time!)
I like ancient history - I have been reading a book about the egyptians which is amazing, one day I'd love to go and see the pyramids!
Disney sounds great, did you go on the rides? I have been to the one in Paris but it was a long time ago. I'm saving to go to Harry Potter studios as those are my favourite books. they have that at Universal too right? Do you like books at all or have a favourite one?
It would be great to get a letter back from you

steph :)

# Cameron & Steph

*Letter 1 - Cameron to Steph*

My name is Cameron and I am a huge Liverpool fan. I have been to a couple of games and love it. I started to play football when I was four and I am now 13. I play for Hibs and am a centre back.

My favourite subject at school is football or P.E. I tend to like any sport I play.

I go to school in Edinburgh but I live in Dunfermline, Fife. So every morning I have to get up at 6.30 to go to school, whereas my brother goes to school in Fife.

I also like to learn about historical events, especially the Romans. I like learning about how people lived.

My favourite place to go is Florida. Disney and Universal. I have also been to Las Vegas and loved it. It was cool to walk through the casinos. We also stayed in the Hard Rock hotel in Vegas before it closed.

*Letter 2 - Steph to Cameron*

Hi Cameron,

Firstly THANKS for your letter!

It sounds like you are really good at football, do you love playing for a team? I have to admit that I don't know much. Is the centre back someone who helps defend? Do you count goals stopped in the same way as goals scored? Is it a position you like?

I have a son who plays football but he is only six – his games are very exciting and the parents are very enthusiastic but most of the goals are scored by chance! There is one kid who often just sits on the floor in front of the goal! What makes Liverpool so good? I have been once but not to the football – would you like to play for them?

I like some sports too – running and swimming and anything outside but I don't do any team sport. Could you recommend something for beginners?

That sounds like a really long way to travel for school, do you mind? I live in Edinburgh too and go to university in Stirling so also have a long way to get there but I don't mind too much as I like listening to music while I drive (or sometimes lectures or homework if I've run out of time!)

I like ancient history – I have been reading a book about the Egyptians which is amazing. One day I'd love to go and see the pyramids!

Disney sounds great, did you go on the rides? I have been to the one in Paris but it was a long time ago. I'm saving to go to Harry Potter Studios as those are my favourite books. They have that at Universal too right? Do you like books at all or have a favourite one? It would be great to get a letter back from you.

Steph :)

---

*Letter 3 - Cameron to Steph*

Dear Steph,

Thank you for your letter.

I love playing for my football team and yes the centre back is the person that is in front of the goalkeeper. We help to stop the goals going in. I love playing in this position.

I also like running and swimming. I find it very relaxing. Also, beginner's badminton is very fun. Do you enjoy university and what music do you like? What are you studying?

I have only seen the first Harry Potter movie and that was a couple of years ago and never got round to watching the rest of them.

I also have a dog. She is a labradoodle called Willow. Do you have any pets and what is your favourite animal?

I have been on a lot of rides at Disney. It was great fun. The Harry Potter area is amazing at Universal. And when I was there I also swam with the dolphins.

I would also love to see the pyramids. I just wonder how they were built back then?

Would love to hear back from you.

From,

Cameron

---

*Letter 4 - Steph to Cameron*

Hi Cameron,

I totally agree with you about swimming and running being relaxing. I am no good at meditation because I don't like to sit still but running always feels a bit like meditating—I can tune the rest of the world out!

Badminton sounds great, have you played before? Do you get time to play other sports or mostly just football? I expect playing on a team takes up a lot of time?

At university I'm studying science and education. I think it's the best course because there is <u>SO</u> much variety. We get to study real practical science classes in physics, maths, chemistry, biology and ecology but at the same time learn about how people learn and how brains and societies work to do that best. I didn't realise university courses could be like this. I thought it would just be 4 years of maths (for example) which I didn't fancy even if I do like the subject.

I can't believe you wrote about your holiday to Disney and didn't mention that there were dolphins—that sounds incredible?! Was it weird to be in the water with them? Was it warm or cold? Do the dolphins come right up? I've only ever seen them from the coast, never up close but they look amazing!

Willow is a great name. I had a cat called Willow when I was a little girl and then I had a house rabbit until very recently. She liked to eat grapes and electrical cables and popcorn! Now I just help my Dad with his dog—a sproodle called Scappa. Scappa is very energetic and incredibly gentle. I take him to the beach sometimes and he runs very fast along the waterline splashing anyone walking too close—he particularly targets anyone standing in the shallows thinking about swimming—soaked!

Are dogs your favourite animal? Or dolphins? Or something else? I think mine are giraffes but I haven't been to see them at the zoo yet.

Write again and tell me about the dolphins if you'd like?

Steph :)

---

*Letter 5 - Cameron to Steph*

Hi Steph

Just want to start by saying I love all the drawings, especially the dolphin. It was very weird being in the water with the dolphins, but also very cold. They have very smooth skin and are very squeaky. We rode on the back of one of them and it dragged us underwater but it was very exciting.

I have played badminton a wee bit, but I'm definitely not a pro. I do sometimes play basketball with my brother, but mostly football. I'm even sometimes the captain - that is also very good.

What is the most exciting thing you have done or been to? Where have you been on holiday? I have also been to New York, and it was amazing seeing the Statue of Liberty.

I do love dogs, but I also like lions. I love animals. My dog is energetic. She loves rolling in the mud and she loves swimming in the sea. My mum loves giraffes as well.

What is your favourite movie? And do you have any other hobbies?

Cameron

---

*Letter 6 - Steph to Cameron*

Hi Cameron,

Firstly I'm glad you like doodles - they sneak into everything I write! Wow the dolphins sound phenomenal but I'm not sure how I feel about being dragged under cold water - very exciting but also like something from a scary film!

Basketball with your brother sounds great, are you close? I don't have any brothers but I do have a sister. We used to play our own version of tennis together in the street outside our house. My dad played/still plays lots of tennis and always wanted us to be good but we preferred making up our own rules to amuse each other. Wow, captain?! That sounds like lots of fun but maybe lots of responsibility. Do you like it?

In response to your question, I think the most exciting place I have ever been is Australia. I went with my cousin and travelled up the east coast from Melbourne - Sydney - Brisbane - Byron Bay - Whitsundays - Cairns in the north with about a thousand stops in between. We got to go snorkelling there which was incredible and then we went to a place called Fraser Island. It has beautiful beaches and lagoons and streams you could swim in but from the shore you could see silhouettes of tiger sharks looming in the breaking waves - so scary! I also held a koala there which was really cute but also really heavy. If you could do anything you've ever dreamed of what would it be?

For movies, I like *Guardians of the Galaxy* because it always makes me laugh. I have been on a real *Avengers* kick lately (apart from *Iron Man* - too boring) I also like *Pan's Labyrinth* - have you seen it? There's a really creepy monster which has eyes in its hands - well worth watching!

I think this might be our last letter for this project but I have really enjoyed writing to you - I'll look out for you in the football in the future Captain Cameron.

Steph :)

---

*Letter 7 - Cameron to Steph*

Hi Steph

I just want to say I have loved writing to you. I have always been close to my brother. We always used to play sport and the Xbox together but not now too much. We do sometimes on the rare occasion.

I love being captain but it is a big responsibility. But I do enjoy it.

Australia sounds amazing. Can't believe you got to go snorkelling in the Great Barrier Reef. It seems you had a great time. I have never heard of Fraser Island but from what you said it sounds breathtaking. I have always wanted to go to Australia but I don't like spiders so I'm not sure if I would cope. But I would love to see a kangaroo. I can't believe you held a Koala. It must be very fluffy and cute.

I do like the Avengers I think my favourite was *Avengers: Endgame*. I have never heard of *Pan's Labyrinth*. I think I will watch it.

Thank you so much for writing to me. I have really enjoyed it.

Cameron

*Letter 8 - Steph to Cameron*

Hi Cameron,

You're right about *Endgame* being one of the best - I love when Thor joins the Guardians! Even though it's clichéd I think my favourite part was the big battle at the end with everyone involved. I think I'm going to go watch it again this weekend.

Oh you should definitely go to Australia if you get a chance - I'm not so keen on spiders either (there was an enormous one in my kitchen the other day - ugh!) but I'm not sure we saw even one in the whole time we were there. It might be over-exaggerated how bad they are - unless you're hiking in the jungle or similar? We didn't actually see kangaroos when I was there but we did see lots of wallabies - they are much smaller and we went to a sanctuary where they were so friendly you could feed them from your palm - like at the deer centre - have you been there?

< This looks like a terrible kangaroo doodle but their legs are actually that weird, you should look up a picture!

This project has been a lot of fun - it is nice to write a proper letter with pen and paper but also strange to get to know someone through writing!

Since this is the last letter I'm going to tell you my favourite bits of our last letters.

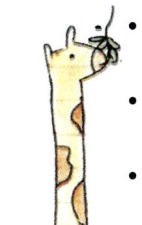

- Hearing about all the sports you play (football is obviously the most important though!)
- Reading about the dolphins in Florida (still not sure how I feel about the cold)
- All the animals - we have talked about dogs, cats, dolphins, giraffes, lions, koalas and now kangaroos - enough for a zoo!

Thanks for writing to me!

Steph :)

Newhaven
Edinburgh

21st September 2021

Dear Charlie,
How are you? Thanks heaps for your excellent letter, great question.

I prefer Scotland, overall, but I still really love Yorkshire (where I grew up) - I like that people chat to each other a bit more there, but Scotland totally feels like home now. *(why do people always draw houses like this, when hardly anyone's house looks like this?)*

And if I could go back in time? Yeah, I'd still be a freelancer. I'd definitely earn more money ($$) doing almost anything else, but I've met some of the most interesting people and got to do some pretty cool stuff. I've got to work in different countries, like Abu Dhabi, Saudi Arabia, the USA & China, and I was living in Vietnam before old Covid arrived. Booo.

Now... onto serious matters...

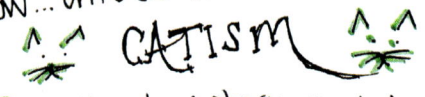

## ^..^ CATISM ^..^

I love all the backstory, and the eternal war against all birds and DEMAND a novel written about it, followed by a Netflix series. At a minimum.

# Charlie & Siân

*Letter 1 - Charlie to Siân*

I like to play video games, watch YouTube and programming in my spare time.

I do Taekwondo twice a week. I'm a yellow stripe about to grade to yellow belt.

My favourite video games are Breath of the Wild, Call of Duty (especially Modern Warfare). I like shooters, open world games.

My favourite school subjects are history, computer science, physics and chemistry

My favourite food is any type of pasta, chicken fajitas, which I like to cook (but nothing else).

I play the electric guitar and I kind of play the piano.

I like a lot of music but my three favourite bands are: Nina, Muse and Radiohead

I have two sisters: Elsie (seven) and Claire (28). Elsie is very, very annoying.

I once ate five plates of Spaghetti: Aglio e Olio with prawns for dinner.

I do Scouts and I am an Assistant Patrol Leader.

My favourite place is my room.

I have a grandparent in Italy, and another in Wales.

My favourite animal are cats. My friend and I started a religion called Catism. I have two cats Major Tom (Tom) and Ziggy Stardust (Ziggy).

I would like to be:

- An IT security analyst (a good hacker)

- A programmer in Web Development or App Development

- Or anything else to do with computers.

My Dad supports Hearts but I only sort of support them.

My mum is English but I am not English at all, 100% Scottish.

---

*Letter 2 - Siân to Charlie*

Dear Charlie,

Hello! My name's Siân (you say it 'Sharn') and I guess I'm your new pen pal.

I really enjoyed reading a bit about you – you have excellent taste in music (<3 Muse, Radiohead & Nirvana too), and it's very cool that you play electric guitar, on top of all the other things you do. I'm learning piano too. We should see if we can both become amazing by Christmas?

Let me tell you a bit about myself then...

I'm a freelancer, which means I do a few different jobs (none of them are hacking though...). My favourite job is writing, but honestly, I mainly email people!  < my working face

I live in Edinburgh. I've been here for about 16 years, but I grew up in York, England. My family are all Welsh, which is why I have the most WELSH NAME EVER.

My parents might as well have named me Dragon Leek.

I did the pen pal project last year, when I was away travelling. Me and my son (who's five now) and his Dad lived in a very small camper van for a few months. It was very fun but oh so smol. *tiny van*

Is there anything else you'd like to know?

I was so impressed with the five plates of spaghetti. Did you get a stomach ache? One Christmas I ate 20 roast potatoes and then had to spend the rest of the day lying down, digesting food like a snake.

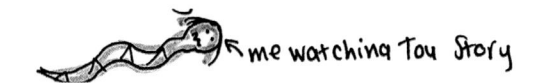

*me watching Toy Story*

Tell me more about Catism!! Are there rules? Do we worship Major Tom and Ziggy? Do we wear tails??

Can't wait to hear from you, have a lovely week.

Siân

If I was a cat, I'd look like this >

*If I was a cat, I think I'd look like this*

---

*Letter 3 - Charlie to Siân*

Hi Sian,

Your letter was very good, I liked all the little pictures.

Do you prefer Scotland or England or are they the same? Do you enjoy your job? If you could go back in time would you still be a freelancer?

In Catism we worship Cat, the creator of everything, and the six demi-cats, who were created by Cat and made the six universes.

We have eternal war against all birds, especially seagulls.

How good are you at piano? How long have you been playing? I've been playing guitar since I was nine, so four years now.

What was your favourite school subject? What's your son called?

I'm writing but I'm not very good at it. I'm good at making stories but when I try to write them they are not very good.

When you were in the campervan, where did you stay?

Have you been anywhere interesting? I've been to Normandy and I go to Wales and Italy a lot because my grandparents live there.

I'm excited to keep talking to you.

Charlie

---

*Letter 4 - Siân to Charlie*

Dear Charlie,

How are you? Thanks heaps for your <u>excellent</u> letter, great questions.

I prefer Scotland, overall, but I still really love Yorkshire (where I grew up)—I like that people chat to each other a bit more there, but Scotland totally feels like home now.

🏠← Why do people always draw houses like this, when hardly anyone's house looks like this?

And if I could go back in time? Yeah, I'd still be a freelancer. I'd definitely earn more money (🤪) doing almost anything else, but I've met some of the most interesting people and got to do some pretty cool stuff. I've got to work in different countries, like Abu Dhabi, Saudi Arabia, the USA and China, and I was living in Vietnam before COVID arrived. Booo :(

   Now … onto serious matters…

    🐱 CATISM 🐱

I <u>love</u> all the backstory, and the eternal war against all the birds, and <u>DEMAND</u> a novel written about it, followed by a Netflix series. At a minimum.

You asked about piano; if I had to explain how good I was in term of an emoji, it would be → 🙂. I really should play more, so I can get better. I reckon that you'd be much better than me after four years.

At school my favourite subject was probably English, but I really enjoyed algebra—I kind of wish I'd done maths for a bit longer, but at my school you had to choose arts (English, history, etc.) or science (maths, chemistry, etc.) when you were 15. I chose arts which means I can …

Read super fast!
Talk about poems for hours!
Never be a doctor! (I didn't really want to be, so that's ok)

You also asked about my son's name? He's called Thane, which I realise is a bit unusual but I love the name. It means 'landkeeper for the King' and has a really interesting history. AND, in Marvel, Thanos's son is called Thane.

I <u>LOVE</u> writing stories, I can totally help get them out of your head and onto the paper! What shall we write a story about?

In the next letter, tell me about your perfect day and about your pals?

Write soon!!

Sian :)

---

*Letter 5 - Charlie to Siân*

Dear Sian,

I started writing Catism's version of the Bible but I stopped. Maybe I'll start writing it again.

All the countries you've been to sound very cool. I'd like to visit Australia but Scotland is very cool.

I like English too but not maths. I'm good at maths, but I find it very boring.

Thane sounds like a cool name. Do you have any pets? Do you watch/play any sports? I play table tennis, and I watch football sometimes but that's it.

Maybe one day I'll write a book about Catism.

If you could be any superhero, which would you be? What TV shows do you watch? What is your favourite movie?

Have you met any famous people? If you could be friends with any person, who would it be?

When you went to China, did you see the Great Wall?

If you could be reincarnated as any animal which would it be?

What's your favourite colour?

!!! VERY IMPORTANT QUESTION !!!

Opinion of pineapple on pizza ???

Hear from you soon,

Charlie

---

*Letter 6 - Siân to Charlie*

Dear Charlie,

Hiya! You should absolutely write more about Catism, you could have so much fun with it.

I'd like to go to Australia too, but I do get worried about the spiders and sharks. I was talking to a pal from Australia, and she said the magpies can get really angry; some times of the year, people have to wear special helmets.

I don't have any pets, and don't really play sports anymore. I like swimming in the sea and running - I used to play hockey and would like to take it up again one day. That's cool that you play table tennis. What's your favourite name for it? Do you prefer

- Table Tennis
- Wiff Waff
- Ping Pong
- OH-NO-WHERE-DID-THE-BALL-GO

(May have made one of these up).

OK, quick fire answer questions…

- If I could be any superhero, I'd be Captain Marvel.
- I like a few TV shows, at the moments it's *Ted Lasso* and *Brooklyn Nine-Nine*.
- My favourite movie is called *Cabaret* - it's a 15 and gets pretty grim but you should watch it when you're 26 and having a bad day.
- I've been lucky to meet a few famous people. In August, I got to interview Cressida Cowell who wrote *How to Train Your Dragon* and she was **so nice** (ASK GERALD IF HE'S MET FAMOUS PEOPLE! He **wins** this question).
- If I could be friends with anyone it would be…hmm. I like funny people so Dan Levy, Aisling Bea and Seth Meyers are all funny famous people I'd like to know.
- I have walked on the Great Wall of China. It was great, lol.
- I would like to be reincarnated as a raccoon, I think. Maybe a fox. Clearly I want to raid bins in my next life.
- Finally *deep breath* this could be a dealbreaker. Charlie, I need to tell you something… I LOVE PINEAPPLE ON PIZZA!!! Controversial, I know. I actually love olives and pineapple on pizza, and I don't like tomato sauce, so my pizzas look weird.

I am so sad this is my last letter, it's been a blast writing to you.

Hope we meet in real life one day. Take care, be kind and continue to be awesome.

Sian

*Letter 7 - Charlie to Siân*

Hi Sian,

Gerald said that you wrote one more letter, but this is my last.

I think the animals in Australia are pretty scary too. I don't really mind spiders normally but the Australian ones are HUGE, and deadly.

One of my friends is very good at swimming, he goes to loads of competitions, and my other friend is third fastest in Scotland for his age.

Table Tennis is the only correct name for it. Except for - OH-NO-WHERE-DID-THE-BALL-GO, I think I might start calling it that.

Captain Marvel is very cool but I think Scarlet Witch or Spider-Man are cooler. Especially the new Miles Morales Spider-Man.

It's cool that you've met Cressida Cowell, but yeah, Gerald has met a LOT of people.

I don't know any of the famous people you said you'd met.

How far along the Great Wall of China did you walk?

I think raccoons are silly but I like foxes.

There's a fox who always sneaks into our garden and then does loads of poos.

I also like pineapple on pizza but the rest of what you have on pizza is weird.

What's your favourite kind of pasta? I like all pasta, but my favourite is either - spaghetti with tomato sauce and meatballs or - spaghetti prawn (*aglio e olio* with prawns)

Hopefully we can meet, Gerald said it might be a while though.

Charlie

*Letter 8 - Siân to Charlie*

Dear Charlie,

CHARLIE – I got it wrong! There *was* an extra letter! I feel like my favourite band finished playing, and they turned the lights on and then SURPRISE ENCORE!  < Me, radiating happiness.

I need to watch new *Spider-Man* ... I think I'm like two Spider-men behind. (Spider-mans? Spider-men?) Fun fact! When Thane (my kid) was a baby, he would randomly scream and yell whenever he saw a picture of Spider-Man. At first I thought it was funny, and then I thought...

"What if my baby is a villain??"

So far, he doesn't seem evil!

I didn't walk super far along the Great Wall of China, maybe 30 minutes there, and 30 minutes walking back. I'm going to my parents' house soon (I call them MamDad), so will try to find the photos for when we meet.

> My MamDad.

Mam = Furious but lovely. Tiny & Welsh.

Dad = Jolly nerd, loves crosswords.

And my favourite type of pasta? Hmm...I'm a bit boring and love green pesto with loads of olives & mushrooms. I'm vegan, so I have the dairy-free stuff... I know that's not for everyone!

moo

When we (eventually) meet in real life, I think we need to discuss…

- Music
- Making up cool stuff
- Food
- How we will SAVE THE WORLD
- Cats

Thanks so much for being my pen pal. When I was 11, I had a French pen pal through my school. Trouble was, I didn't know much French and she didn't know much English, so our letters were always <u>very</u> short. You are an excellent pen pal and I'll look forward to seeing you in 3D.

< An example. (I don't even like tennis)

Be safe, be kind

Sian

# Daniel & Will

*Letter 1 - Daniel to Will*

Like Rubik's cubes, video games, talking to my friends, reading and Pokemon.

I play football, judo and basketball.

My favourite TV show is the *Goldbergs*, which is about a family in the '80s.

My favourite food is sausage because it tastes amazing, veggie sausage is all right.

I like Avicii.

My favourite subject is P.E. or science.

My favourite video game is *Hollow Knight* and my favourite book is the *Frostheart*.

I live with my mum, no siblings and I spend a lot of time with my granny.

I like Marvel and my favourite superhero is Wolverine.

I like fantasy and adventure books.

I don't like sleeping.

My favourite place is Florida because of the theme parks.

I want to go to Japan because it looks futuristic and there are lots of Pokemon related things.

*Letter 2 - Will to Daniel*

Hi Daniel,

My name is Will. Unfortunately I am not a famous musician like Avicii, just an old Grandad. Hopefully if we write to each other you can tell me all sorts of things which I can share with my grandchildren and look a bit cooler. Thanks for the sheet you wrote about the things you like to do. It sounds like you have a busy time.

Can you complete the Rubik's cube? I would be really impressed if you could. Rubik invented the cube when I was about 20 years old and I could never master it. I always ended up getting really frustrated so I'm glad you enjoy it. Because I couldn't do it properly I did a magic trick switching the unfinished cube for a complete one I had hidden in my pocket. It looked like I was good at it until a mate saw me making the switch!

You are lucky to have good video games to play. We just had a simple one with no graphics, where you just had to shoot little dots before they shot you. It was revolutionary at the time.

I am having to learn a little more about video games as my daughter works for PlayStation. Perhaps you can tell me about *Hollow Knight* and why it is your favourite game? I can then tell her so she gets it featured on PlayStation. Which console do you use? If you like Pokemon, I guess it is probably Nintendo?

It's a shame we can't come into school at the moment because of the COVID virus but perhaps it will change by Christmas. But if you can't get together, letters are a great way of sharing thoughts and ideas. How did you manage with lockdown? You must have missed your friends and playing football?

I'm quite lucky because I have a dog to keep me company and we walked for miles and miles. I was a bit annoyed because I realised that in three months I had walked so much that if it had been in a straight line I could have been in Paris. That would have been fun. You couldn't walk to Florida but is there anywhere in the world you would have liked to have reached?

My dog is called Seve, after a famous golfer called Seve Ballesteros. I have never heard of another dog called Seve, have you? What is the oddest name for an animal you have heard? (Here is a Grandad joke for you - What did you call a penguin in the Sahara desert? Lost)

We called the dog Seve as my daughter thought the dog and the golfer were both good looking, so the name stuck.

He is never without a ball and can find it even if I throw it into the deepest jungle. He sniffs it out. As soon as he gets the scent his tail starts to wag at the speed of light. I know he is going to appear with the ball in his mouth looking very pleased with himself. I wish I had known he was so good when he was younger. I could have trained him as a sniffer dog.

Did you know some dogs have been trained to sniff out the COVID virus? They are being used at some airports to prevent people coming into the country with COVID.

It's good that you can spend time with your Gran. She will enjoy your company. Does she let you get away with things your Mum wouldn't? I enjoy the company of my grandchildren. They make me laugh but they live in London and Canada so I haven't seen them much. My youngest grandson was born eight days ago so I hope to meet him soon.

We are pretty different in our ideas about sleep. I love it, but at your age there are so many exciting things to do so sleeping can feel like a waste of time!

I'm looking forward to hearing about some of the things getting you excited now and those 'cool' things I can tell my grandchildren.

All the best for now

Will

*Letter 3 - Daniel to Will*

Hi Will,

How are you? How has your week been? I've heard that you travelled the world selling sausage skins. Are there different kinds of sausage skins? I love sausages. Where did you go selling sausage skins?

I can solve a Rubik's cube in 20 seconds. Maybe in the future I can get a lot better and go to competitions. What I like about *Hollow Knight* is that the art style is simplistic yet so detailed at the same time. It is also my favourite game because of the backstory and all the different game mechanics.

My favourite console is the Nintendo Switch. I do have a PS5 as well which I got for Christmas last year.

Lockdown was fine but I really missed my friends and school was a lot harder when we were using Teams to communicate. How did you cope with lockdown?

I would like to go to Skye. I went there last year during Easter with my Mum.

Seve sounds like a nice dog. What breed is he? I have a cat called Nala. I've had her for eight years now but she is a tiny cat. My Granny also has a dog called Chloe who is a greyhound.

I've got to go but will try to answer the rest of your questions on my next letter.

Best regards

Daniel

*Letter 4 - Will to Daniel*

Hi again Daniel,

What a great letter. You gave me so much to think about.

My week has been pretty exhausting. I've been down to London to visit my daughter and her new baby. He is my sixth grandchild. I was babysitting for a couple of days. I forgot how exhausting small kids are. Seb, who is two, just didn't stop 24 hours a day and babies do cry quite a lot in the middle of the night. I'm now on the train going home to Edinburgh but it has just broken down. I'm typing this letter because if I tried to write it on the train, which is very shoogly, the writing would be so bad you would think it was done by an alien and have no idea what I was writing.

Yes I had this very odd job selling sausage skins! There are lots and lots of different types and we sold about £300 million worth every year which is a lot. I was so lucky I visited nearly 60 countries because, like you, people all over the world love sausages. My favourite countries were Colombia in South America and Taiwan in the Far East. Both were beautiful and strange. I had to eat snake in Taiwan and met some kidnappers in Colombia (lucky they didn't try to kidnap me).

Twenty seconds for the Rubik's cube. Wow, that is brilliant. Are you the fastest in your school? Perhaps you could start a school competition and win, showing everyone how good you are? Would be good practice for a bigger competition.

Yes, Teams is quite difficult. Communication isn't the same when it is through a screen. I did some teaching using Teams in lockdown. I didn't like it much. Yuk! I was lucky with lockdown because I have a garden and the dog but there are lots of things we all missed. We will just have to try to make up for it now by seeing friends as much as possible and catching up on all that missed school time. I'm still doing tests for research on COVID every month. The worst bit is I have to stab my own finger to give blood to test and I'm a real coward so it takes ages as I try to stab my finger with my eyes shut.

I haven't been to Skye for a long, long time but loved it when I was there. I think Easter would be a great time to go as the midges wouldn't be out in force. Do you like the outdoors? There are fantastic wild places in Skye which can make you think you are in a different world, and you can look at things from a completely different point of view. I like getting away from lots of people and feeling the wind (and Scottish rain) on my face.

Seve is a retriever. He's small for the breed, like your cat Nala, and I keep him on quite a strict diet because Retrievers tend to get fat and I don't think that would be good for him. When I'm away from home he stays with my neighbour who feeds him lots and lots. I suspect he prefers to be there because when I get home he goes back on a diet and I can also be quite grumpy. He is lovely and great fun. I thought he was quite fast, running on the beach down at North Berwick but your granny's dog would beat him so easily he would be really embarrassed.

How is school going? Do you have a favourite subject or a favourite teacher? Or do you just like them all? I liked Science at school with weird experiments even though I could never get them to work out. A bit like Hogwarts pupils in the Harry Potter books.

My daughter will try to get you a special code for your PlayStation which would allow you to get some games for free. She sent me a couple of games but they are for PS4 so unfortunately won't work. I'm hoping she can get the code. Can you check with your mum that she is happy for me to send you the game codes and let me know in the next letter? I need to know that your mum has said yes before I can send something. I haven't got the codes yet so perhaps it won't happen but if I do get them, I will send them to you. (Fingers crossed). She said that she liked *Hollow Knight* too.

All the best,

Will

*Letter 5 - Daniel to Will*

Hi Will,

Sorry to hear your week's been exhausting, but it must have been nice to see your family. My mum said I was a handful when I was a baby. What did you do on the train home other than writing the letter?

Did you ever get free sausages? If you did, I might consider getting that job when I'm older, but I might get homesick a lot. Also what did the snake taste like? How did you know that in Colombia they were kidnappers?

I think I'm the fastest at my school at solving the Rubik's cube. Maybe when COVID dies down a lot more I would be able to start a Rubik's cube club (with competitions as well).

Who were you teaching in lockdown? One of the worst things for me with lockdown was not seeing my friends, so I'm glad school is back. I would be just the same if I had to prick my finger, especially when you have to do it yourself and not get someone to do it for you.

I like the outdoors, because it's really relaxing (especially in the woods). I also like walking through shallow streams and hopping from one rock to the other. When I was in Skye, I went to see the fairy pools, which were amazing.

I don't know if my granny's dog would beat Seve because she is an ex-racer and has hurt her shoulder, but she is getting better. But Chloe is still really fast when my granny gets home from being out on a walk, and just runs around my granny's house.

School's good. My favourite subject is History and one of my favourite teachers is Mr Brown, who I think you've met before. I still enjoy most subjects.

I'm at school writing this letter so I can't ask her about the code but I'm sure she would be fine with it. You are actually able to play PS4 games on PS5 as well. Your daughter must have quite a high-up job if she can give away free codes?

It's been really nice to write letters to you and I'm sad I can't write any more after this. Hopefully we can meet one day and I can show you my Rubik's cube.

Best wishes,

Daniel

---

*Letter 6 - Will to Daniel*

Good morning Daniel.

Hope you are having a good day. Thanks again for a great letter. I'm being lazy again and typing this. I've always got an excuse. This time it is a bit close to the deadline for getting the letter to you before your class and I am much quicker with typing than writing.

I watched a movie on the train which I had downloaded. It was a Sky special about a mother and daughter who were assassins. I enjoyed it and found it funny, but it was very violent at times and I did worry that I was laughing while there were shootings and all the other stuff.

Glad you like Mr Brown. I think he is a very good teacher and cares for his students and their success. I have done a few sessions with the Super Power Agency with Mr Brown in the past and hope we will be able to get back into the school at some stage in the future.

I bet you were a handful when you were a baby. Most babies are. Since I've been back from my babysitting, I've been quite busy. I went to see a play. They have a really good offer on at the moment where you get a pie, a pint and a play. The play was about a girl footballer from Glasgow called Rose Reilly. Have you heard of her? I hadn't and I don't think many people have but she should be a Scottish hero. She was amazing. She won the league title in France and in Italy in the same year playing in Italy on a Saturday and France on a Sunday. She was

European Footballer of the Year on at least two occasions and, although she was pure Scottish, she managed to play for Italy in the World Cup and scored a goal in the final when they beat Germany. Despite all this the SFA banned her for life because, before she went abroad, she played in a match for a Scottish team against England when the SFA said girls couldn't play football. She scored against England from a corner!

I've bought myself a new battery lawnmower and have at last cut my grass. I can never decide whether I can just leave the grass to grow and get all sorts of wildlife or cut it so that it looks neater. With the new mower I've got no real excuse not to cut it.

My son in Canada got a puppy this week. It is an Aussiedoodle –which I had never heard of. Have you? They have called it Harry. Can you guess why? Here is a hint: it has a white flash on his head which is shaped like a lightning bolt. The breed is known as the Einstein of dogs because apparently they are very clever but I know they can't do a Rubik's cube. Great to hear that Chloe is getting better.

Yes, I did get free sausages! It was great on summer weekends. We had a test centre where they made sausages and I would ask them to make me special flavours and types for barbecuing if the weather was going to be nice. My favourites were Frankfurters with cheese. The cheese melted inside the sausage on the barbecue and they were brilliant. They tasted much better than the snake in Taiwan! I pretended it tasted like chicken because I didn't want to think too much about it but actually it wasn't too bad, more like fish than chicken. I was with my distributor in Colombia, who helped me build business there, who knew the men in this remote pub we were at. Talking to them they said they were fishermen but there wasn't anywhere to fish. They explained that they were fishers for men. They put up roadblocks and saw what swam in. They stole or kidnapped or let people go depending on the situation. I don't think they were kidding because they had guns. I'm just glad my distributor knew them. I was pretty scared.

The teaching I was doing during lockdown was for young people starting a business. I was helping them to find ways to sell more product or to market their product more efficiently. So many people have been starting new businesses because they couldn't get out to their jobs. Lots of people took the opportunity to try and make their dreams into a business. People had so many great ideas - a drone pilot helping farmers count sheep on the hill or inspecting roofs, a brewery, vegan cake maker, glass blower, coffee roaster, joiner, plumber. All sorts of fascinating business ideas. Some of them are doing really well and making a good living – which is great. What sort of business would you think of starting? Hard work but fabulous if you can succeed.

I've never been to the Fairy Pools in Skye. That is a fantastic thing to have seen and to have locked into your memories. Rock jumping is great. Have you ever tried canyoning? It's a bit like jumping from rock to rock. If you ever get a chance, perhaps once COVID dies down, the school might do trips to outdoor centres. Canyoning is when you clamber up or down a stream or river getting to the destination anyway you can jumping, clambering, swimming, abseiling, shooting rapids. Someone suggested I try and I thought that sounds miserable! It was brilliant. You wouldn't believe how exciting it can be.

My daughter has come up trumps (I think!). She is pretty senior at PlayStation, one of the commercial directors, so she can sometimes manage to get things.

Here is a code for the new *FIFA* game. It only came out on Friday so not many people will have it. XXXX-XXXX-XXXX (It will only work once so keep it safe until you get back home). I hope it loads successfully and that it is good fun.

I've enjoyed writing these letters and hearing the things that interest you. I think we might be having a get together of letter writers (outside) in October which would be good. I would like to see you complete the cube. If you can beat your record time I'll bring you the PS4 games!

All the best,

Will

# Dee & Martin

*Letter 1 - Dee to Martin*

Dear Martin,

Hi, my name is Dee. I'm 13 years old. I go to Broughton High School. I'm in S2. I like to write stories. I like to play my PC. I like to watch Netflix—right now I'm watching *Atypical*.

I wanted to ask you some questions. Hope that's OK. 😊

First I would like to ask if you have a job? Where is your favourite place to go in the world, or somewhere you would like to go?

How old are you? What's your favourite movie series or book?

What was your week/weekend like? Hope it was good. I hope to hear from you soon.

I have to go but I'm excited to hear from you.

Bye Martin.

Dee

*Letter 2 - Martin to Dee*

Dear Dee,

It is great to meet you. Thank you so much for writing to me.

I loved your questions. Here are my answers:

My Job

My job is to help people with social media. I help businesses and charities decide what to say on their social media profiles. I used to work at Young Scot, then started my own company eight years ago. I also do some writing for people, mostly for websites.

My Favourite Place

This one is hard! I love living in Edinburgh, so it is one of my favourite places. I also have friends who live right on the river on the east coast of the USA, and it is one of my favourite places to visit.

One place I have never been to but would love to see is New Zealand. It looks beautiful.

My Age

I turned 45 last Thursday. But I always feel a lot younger than that!

My Favourite Books, Series or Movie

Another tough one to answer. I could give you lots of choices for this one. I'll put some I enjoyed recently.

I grew up reading comic books, and watch the Marvel films with my niece and nephews. We are all looking forward to the new Spider-Man film at Christmas.

One of my favourite TV shows is *Taskmaster*. I'm not sure how well I would do with tasks if I had to do them though.

My weekend was good thank you. We were in the Scottish Borders. My wife and I took our son Jacob (he is two and a half) to see his grandparents. They live in the countryside, with not many houses nearby, so he can run around happily.

You said you like to play on your PC. What games do you play? I have an Xbox that I play on sometimes.

I haven't seen *Atypical* but I will need to check it out now you have recommended it. I have been looking for new things to watch. Is there anything else that you have really liked?

What kind of stories do you like writing? Do you like reading stories too?

Thanks again for the letter. Look forward to hearing from you.

Martin

P.S. Sorry about the handwriting! It has never been any good.

---

*Letter 3 - Dee to Martin*

Dear Martin,

Thank you for your questions and letter.

I find it great that you help people. Since you live in Edinburgh, I have probably seen you around. Where do you live in Edinburgh? That sounds creepy. 😂 That's supposed to be laughing. My pal is from New Zealand.

I never thought you would be 45. Happy late birthday. I am only 13.

When I heard you watched Marvel movies I was so happy. I can't wait for *Spider-Man*. I grew up watching it. Andrew Garfield is probably the best Peter Parker. Tom Holland is also very good.

You weekend sounded good. I love your son's name. What is your wife's name?

I mostly play *Minecraft*. *Atypical* is also good.

I normally write horror stories.

Thank you for your letter.

Dee. 😃

Also, don't worry about your handwriting.

# Emma!

Hi Emma! I can't quite believe this is our last letter. I've really been enjoying hearing your news. I wonder how you got on at the dance competition on Saturday. It's so brave that you dance solo. I'd love to hear about the different routines you performed for each section.

You mentioned that you love Autumn and Winter. I also love seeing the seasons change. My brother lives in Singapore* where it is constantly hot and humid! They get amazing thunderstorms sometimes with enormous bolts of lightning that light up the whole room at night. But it never snows. I do appreciate the variety of weather we get in Scotland. Right now Alvie and I are wearing matching jeans and jumpers and we are going to the cinema. I love to watch lots of movies in the autumn.

Hopefully I will get to meet you in person soon. That would be really brilliant.

Have an excellent weekend-

Your penpal

Claire

(and little Mr Alvie)

# Emma & Claire S

*Letter 1 - Emma to Claire*

Dear Claire,

Hi, my name is Emma. I am 13 years old and I am from Edinburgh. My favourite thing to do is dance. I go to a dance school called DN Dance. I also do competitions on the weekend.

I perform six dances. My favourite one is my ballet solo because I got a brand new tutu last week. It is red with glitter. I also like to play golf. I go to a golf course with my dad and he helps me be a better golfer.

I love animals. I have a dog called Honey and she is a Labrador. I am also an only child. I have no siblings, it's just me, my mum and my dad.

When I am older I would love to be a professional dancer and travel the world but I would also love to be a pilot. I love planes and I would really love to travel the world.

My favourite food is pizza and ice cream.

I can't wait to read your letter and get to know you.

From Emma

*Letter 2 - Claire to Emma*

Hi Emma,

Thank you so much for your letter. It was brilliant reading about your hobbies and interests.

Guess what? I also love dancing! I used to do ballet and tap lessons when I was wee. I went to a place in Edinburgh called Rebecca Walker Dance School. I remember how exciting it was preparing for an annual dance show at Church Hill Theatre. I was three (I think) when I did my first one. I can remember getting fitted for tutus and someone putting lipstick and hairspray on me before the show!

Your dog Honey sounds cute. Have you ever seen the old adverts for Andrex toilet paper with a Labrador puppy? ( I'm sure they will be on YouTube!)

I don't have pets... but I do have a new baby. My son Alvie was born on May 30th this year and he is very sweet. He's chatting away in baby language right now.

You mentioned that you love travelling - me too. Where would be your favourite place to go? Do you also have a favourite place in Scotland?

I'm really looking forward to your next letter. Let me know what you have been up to.

Bye for now!

Claire

*Letter 3 - Emma to Claire*

Hi Claire!

Thank you for your letter. I loved hearing that you did dancing too. Also I have seen the advert for Andrex toilet paper—my dog looks like that puppy but her fur is more golden, that's why we call her Honey.

You asked me some questions about travelling. My favourite place to go is Orlando, Florida. I love going to Disney World there. What is your favourite place to go?

I also liked reading about your son—he sounds so cute.

Last weekend I had a dance competition called CYD and I got a scholarship for a dance convention next year which I am really excited about. What did you do at the weekend? I'm reading this book called *The Martian* which is based on the movie. It is so good. I have seen the movie so many times because my dad loves space.

I have also got some random questions like what is your favourite food and what's one place you would love to go?

I'm really excited to read the next letter!!!

Bye,

Emma

---

*Letter 4 - Claire to Emma*

Hi Emma

CONGRATULATIONS!

Wow that is super good news about the dance competition next year! Well done you. Exciting times indeed. You must have danced your wee socks off.

You asked me what my favourite food is.... it's hard to narrow it down as I love so many. Pepperoni pizza with pineapple always hits the spot. Although some people find pineapple a controversial topping.

You also asked me where I would like to travel to. Again so many options as I love to travel. One day I would like to see Japan. Or Yosemite Park in America. My brother lives in Singapore with his wife and my nephew so maybe sometime I'll be able to visit them with my baby Alvie. Last week I got as far as exotic Glasgow.

It's great that you are loving the book *The Martian*. It's an amazing feeling when you find a book you can really get into. It's also cool that you and your dad both love space! Have you ever been to the planetarium at Dynamic Earth?

I'll be sad when our letters are over - it's really fun hearing from you! Let me know your news from this week and bye for now.

Claire (and Alvie snoring next to me Zzzzzz)

---

*Letter 5 - Emma to Claire*

Hi Claire!

I love reading your letters. I have actually never tried pineapple on pizza, but I would love to try.

I have actually been to Dynamic Earth. I went for a primary school trip, and my eighth birthday was actually there. I don't think I have been to the planetarium, but I would love to go.

This weekend I actually have another dance competition. It's called VAD and I'm really nervous. I'm doing two of my solos on Saturday and have my duet and groups on Sunday. So I am hoping to get a trophy, but I'm up against a lot of people.

I'm also really happy because I love autumn and winter. I don't know why, because I just moan about how it rains and it's cold, but I just love it. (What is your favourite season?)

I also had a science and history test last week. I got 95% in history, but I only got 68% on my science. I was a bit sad about that.

I'll be really sad when our letters are over. I have really enjoyed reading them. Let me know what you did this week.

Thank you so much for writing me letters.

Bye,

Emma

---

*Letter 6 - Claire to Emma*

Hi Emma!

I can't quite believe this is our last letter. I've really enjoyed hearing your news. I wonder how you got on in the dance competition on Saturday? It's so brave that you dance solo. I'd love to hear about the different routines you performed for each section.

You mentioned that you love autumn and winter. I also love seeing the seasons change. My brother lives in Singapore* where it is constantly hot and humid! They get amazing thunderstorms sometimes with enormous bolts of lightning that light up the whole room at night. But it never snows. I do appreciate the variety of weather we get in Scotland. Right now Alvie and I are wearing matching jeans and jumpers and we are going to the cinema. I love to watch lots of movies in the autumn.

Hopefully I will get to meet you in person soon. That would be really brilliant.

Have an excellent weekend.

Your pen pal

Claire (and little Mr Alvie)

* Sorry for this scribble. Alvie kicked me! 😀

# Ethan & Elaine

*Letter 1 - Ethan to Elaine*

I like video games and reading.

I like to swim.

I don't like TV.

I like superheroes.

I like bacon and cheeseburgers and pepperoni pizza.

My favourite video game is FPS, space and factory/automat.

I like music.

My favourite subject is P.E. because it's fun to run around.

I am introverted.

My favourite dessert is ice cream and fudge.

I am 13.

I broke the 12 year old record in my swim team.

My favourite place in the world is Maui because of all the beauty and wildlife.

I like to bake.

*Letter 2 - Elaine to Ethan*

Dear Ethan G,

It's so nice to hear your likes and interests in your introduction. I have so many questions I'd like to ask you, to find out more about you.

But first... a little about me.

I was not much good at P.E. I didn't like it at school like you do. I liked art, English, history and science...mainly biology. I have always enjoyed reading, writing stories and sometimes poetry. When my brain is tired poems are soothing and help me imagine other worlds and feel different emotions.

What do you like about reading?

My superpower is real.... Yoga.

It makes me calm when I am anxious and my body strong. Sometimes I feel like a giant after Yoga. Strange but true.

WHAT IS YOUR SUPERPOWER?

I would love to understand more about video games. What does FDS mean? Can you give me examples of "Space +factory" and "automation" games. These didn't exist when I was young!

You are a pretty amazing swimmer to have the 12 year old record for fifty metre front crawl. How often do you swim?

I LOVE TO TRAVEL. I HAVE NEVER BEEN TO HAWAII - Maui is an island in Hawaii isn't it? Tell me what kind of wildlife you saw there?

I HAVE BEEN TO AUSTRALIA and NEW ZEALAND WHICH IS "QUITE" CLOSE TO HAWAII. ARE THERE CREATURES WHICH EXIST ON MAUI and nowhere else?

I have a big dog called Red. Do you have any pets?

Thanks for your next letter in advance.

Bye for now. Yours faithfully Elaine.

---

*Letter 3 - Ethan to Elaine*

Dear Elaine,

I'm glad to get to know you! I have some questions I want to ask you but first I will be answering yours.

Now my handwriting is a bit funky so you might not understand some of the things I write. I've never been one to like drawing and writing, I'm more of a puzzle solver. I quite like history and science as well, but chemistry is my favourite. I really like fantasy and magic books because they spark my imagination.

I am a social introvert, I can talk easily with close friends but find it harder to talk to people I don't really know which is why I like playing video games because it's easier to socialise with them. One type of game I like playing is FPS, or first-person shooters. For one, I have to really concentrate to get things done. An old factory game on the computer is called *Factorio*, where you build machines that can create things that go into other machines, without me having to do anything which creates automation!

I have more to talk about but not enough time!

From your new pen pal,

Ethan G.

*Letter 4 - Elaine to Ethan*

Dear Pen Pal Ethan,

Lovely to read your latest letter. And I can read it. My son's writing is very similar to yours. He is out in the world now and has just been working on a production of *The Lark*... which is based on a video game, I believe.

I like the word 'Funky' to describe your writing! I had a friend who wrote the letter 'a' like this and I thought it was so cool I taught myself how to do it and now I can't stop!

Now I see I misread FPS for FDS! Thanks for explaining it as 'First Person Shooter'. Now I understand. I suppose it's fun hooking up with friends and playing these games. It's almost like being together without having to be outside. I really like going out to the seaside or the forest and walking in the wind and rain, if I have to. I prefer rain to wind. There is a word derived from Greek called 'Petrichor' which means the earthy scent produced when rain falls on dry soil. What an amazing word... and an incredibly evocative smell. I love it. That's why I go into the park and out into the woods, even amongst the trees at the side of the road you can smell it. Sometimes it's mingled with dog wee!! I really like Tyninghame beach and forest.

Do you have a favourite outdoor place?

I know you don't get a lot of time in class to write your response so I will keep this brief.

I look forward to hearing more about you.

Your pen pal, Elaine.

*Letter 5 - Ethan to Elaine*

Dear Elaine,

How are you doing? My letters may be shorter because I'm not very good at starting letters.

What is your favourite book/series/author?

Mine is Rain Oxford and Leigh Bardugo. The first one made the Elemental Series and the Guardian series, and the second one made the Grisha series which is now a Netflix series.

Not many games I play are multi-player because everyone uses consoles (Xbox, PlayStation) while I play on a computer. I've never really liked the outside and would rather play video games because I need to keep my hands busy. I would also prefer the rain than the wind because the wind would penetrate my jumper. What's your normal attire? I usually wear sweatpants, a tee-shirt and a jumper which is usually enough.

I haven't heard of *The Lark* but it sounds like a horror film/game. Do you play any board or card games? I play many board games, the most recent game I started playing was the digital version of *Gloomhaven*. *Gloomhaven* is a legacy game that can only be played once, but since I have the digital version I can play it as many times as I want.

I have to go now. Have a good week!

Ethan G

---

*Letter 6 - Elaine to Ethan*

Dear Ethan G,

I am well thank you. I am about to go on a road trip to Wales with a friend and stay in a barn for three days on Mount Snowdon. I hope we don't run out of petrol ... ha ha. It is difficult to know how to start a letter, but there, it's done.

I don't know the series you have mentioned but I will check out The Elemental, Guardian and Grisha series.

My favourite authors are Ian McEwan, Margaret Atwood and Maggie O'Farrell at the moment. It changes. The only series based on a book by one of these authors was *The Handmaid's Tale*. It's about making women have babies by M Atwood.

I usually wear jeans and a jumper or shirt or a dress so that I don't have to decide what matches my jeans or trousers. I like wearing shoes I can run in.

The only games I play are Backgammon, Chess - I am only learning - and Scrabble.

I find card games a little tedious but play them with people who like playing them.

I think this is our last letter so I wish you all the best and hope you have a great year. If it is not the last time, please tell me about what you'd like to do in the Christmas holidays.

Take care,

Elaine

---

*Letter 7 - Ethan to Elaine*

Dear Elaine,

I hope your trip goes well and the fuel shortage does not end it early. I've never been one to travel. They can be uncomfortable at times. How long is a long drive to you? I have heard that an hour is a long drive for some people. It will be very exciting to meet you!

I feel like I've heard of M Atwood and the *Handmaid's Tale* seems more like a mystery novel. Chess has always been a fun game, but Scrabble can be very hard since you really have to know the whole English dictionary.

I like card games depending on what it's about, for instance there is a game called *Star Wars: Outer Rim* where it has some cardboard cutouts with lots of cards. I just like many board games but I have a hard time staying with one thing.

This is our last letter and I wonder when we will meet and finally see each other!

Best regards, Ethan

Edinburgh
15/09/21

Hello Harrison,

I'm Claire, I am your new pen pal! Have you ever had a pen pal before? I always had a pen pal when I was growing up. But I suppose we didn't [...]

I have [...] hear more [...] you're from [...] now? I [...] like you [...] have nev[...] I have [...] also w[...]

I have googled [...] so ne[...] know [...] on N[...] than [...] so [...]

Science is great! Have you been to Dynamic Earth in Edinburgh?

Wow £57 is lots - did you buy more toys with it? I used to sell my old toys to buy new ones when I was younger. Don't think I ever made £57 though.

What did you do for your birthday this year? My birthday is on 13th January. It's always very cold on my Birthday. This year I went for a walk in the snow with my dog.

My Dog (Nelly) is my best friend. She is 7 years old and her birthday is on 15th October.

This is her and her dog friend Alba.....

Alba is a king charles cavalier spaniel.

She is smiling

Do you like dogs?

Look forward to getting your letter.

From, Claire

# Harrison & Claire H

*Letter 1 - Harrison to Claire*

I'm 13.

I like the TV show and toy *Beyblade Burst*.

I like Rubik's cubes. I can solve it, I have solved it over 20 times.

I like series on Netflix. They need to release four seasons because I need something to watch.

I love science.

My favourite food is the chicken noodle soup my mum makes.

I'm from the Philippines, Dipolog city.

I sell my old toys like Pokémon cards, Power Rangers, Bionicles... I made over £51 in one week.

On car rides I like to look out the window and imagine the clouds are in a war.

If I had to go anywhere in the world it would be Japan because of Beyblades and I've been there before, but I was only three to four and there's so much more to explore.

*Letter 2 - Claire to Harrison*

Hello Harrison,

I'm Claire, your new pen pal!

Have you ever had a pen pal before? I always had a pen pal when I was growing up. But I suppose we didn't have mobile phones like now.

I have read through your bio, it was great to hear more about you. Firstly, that is so cool that you're from the Philippines - do you go there often now? I have never been but I would love to go. I, like you, would also really like to visit Japan. I have never been there either. My favourite place I have visited was Sydney in Australia. I would also like to visit New Zealand.

I have never heard of *Beyblade Burst* - I just googled it. I will watch it at the weekend though so next time we speak I will be able to let you know if I like it too. I love watching things on Netflix too! I think I like TV series more than films - what about you?

<u>SO COOL</u> that you can solve a Rubik's Cube - I would love to learn how to do it.

Science is great! Have you been to Dynamic Earth in Edinburgh?

WOW £51 is lots - did you buy more toys with it? I used to sell my old toys to buy new ones when I was younger. Don't think I ever made £51 though.

What did you do for your birthday this year? My birthday is 13th January. It's always been very cold on my birthday. This year I went for a walk in the snow with my dog.

My dog Nelly is my best friend. She is seven years old and her birthday is on 15th October.

This is her and her dog friend Alba.

> Alba is a King Charles cavalier spaniel.
> She is smiling
> Do you like dogs?

Do you like dogs?

Look forward to getting your letter.

From, Claire

---

*Letter 3 - Harrison to Claire*

Hello Claire,

No, I never had a pen pal, you're my first one. Well, I used to write letters to my friend. Sorry if I'm writing too far apart, it is just how I like writing. I don't often go to the Philippines, it costs a lot of money.

I hope you like *Beyblade* and watch it in English. It's a Japanese series which I like. But if you want to watch it, it is all up to you. Your dog looks so happy. I love dogs.

My birthday is on March 23, if I didn't mention it. If I did sorry I would like to know you more. When I read you're watching *Beyblade*, it made me so happy. No one I know likes *Beyblade* except my friend Jonald.

Jonald is my friend. His birthday is the day after mine - March 24. We're the same age, 13, love the same stuff. We kind of look the same, we're both from the Philippines, we're basically twins.

Hope to know more about you and one day I hope I can meet you and your dog.

From, Harrison

*Letter 4 - Claire to Harrison*

Hello Harrison,

Thank you for your letter! I really liked reading it. Are you enjoying having your first pen pal? I think it's really fun.

Don't worry about your handwriting - I decided to type my letter this week. Do you think I should type or handwrite them from now on? I think I might like handwriting them better.

I liked *Beyblade* actually. I watched it in English. Maybe this week I could try and watch the Japanese version. I will let you know whether I like that. You, me and Jonald could have a chat about *Beyblade* together one day! Have you got any other recommendations for me?

I think I would like to go to the cinema soon too. I haven't been in so long and I miss it. I miss the Tango ice blasts and the pick and mix too. Do you like the cinema?

Ah, I am happy you like my dog, Nelly. She is the best. She was very happy that day as we were walking in the Highlands and that's one of her favourite things. She also LOVES the beach and will run in the water after her ball for hours. I take her to the beach most days as I don't live very far away. On the weekends I take her to different places too. I like going to North Berwick. What are your favourite places in Scotland? I think Edinburgh is such a great place to live! I hope you like it here too.

What are your favourite foods? I just had a pizza delivery for dinner and it was so delicious. I think pizza is my favourite food. And maybe mashed potatoes.

I look forward to your next letter and I hope you've had a great week!

From, Claire and Nelly the Dog

*Letter 5 - Harrison to Claire*

Hi Claire,

I'm so happy you liked my letter. I think you should hand-write it if you like.

I am so, so, so, so happy you like *Beyblade* on Netflix. You can watch the Japanese version on YouTube. If you're going to watch the Japanese version, watch *Beyblade DB* episode 1–26. Episode 26 is coming out tomorrow 25/9/21. It just makes my day that you watch *Beyblade*. My favourite foods are my mum's chicken noodle soup or pizza. Hope you feel better next week. Hope your dog Nelly has a good week.

From, Harrison

P.S. Who's your favourite character in *Beyblade* so far? My favourite character is Aiger from *Beyblade Burst Turbo* on Netflix.

---

*Letter 6 - Claire to Harrison*

Hi Harrison,

Thanks for your letter! What have you been up to this week?

So, Nelly and I watched *Beyblade DB* episode 26 like you suggested. I have taken a little photo of her watching it - she had a little snack while she watched. Did you enjoy the episode? What was your favourite part?

I like this character - who is that? I don't know their names. Do you like this character?

How long have you been watching *Beyblade* for?

I have had a good week. Unfortunately, I have been isolating so I have had lots of time to read and cook but mostly I have been watching TV.

I have watched lots of things on Netflix and keep asking my friends for new recommendations as I have run out. I am looking forward to being able to go to the beach at the weekend though. What do you like to do at the weekend? Do you have any hobbies? And are you a member of any teams and clubs?

I love autumn, do you? What is your favourite time of the year? I like summer and autumn the best I think.

Your mum's chicken noodle soup sounds lovely. My mum cooks a very nice roast dinner so I enjoy that when I go and see her. My mum doesn't live in Edinburgh though so I don't see her loads. Nelly likes my mum's roast dinner too, especially the chicken.

Speak soon,

Claire and Nelly the Dog

---

*Letter 7 - Harrison to Claire*

Hi Claire,

My week was good. I was sick on Monday.

What did you think about episode 26? Your favourite character was killed (Bell). I've been watching *Beyblade* for six years. Now you should watch *Beyblade* DB episodes 27 and 28. My favourite part is when Bell's Beyblade turns gold. It was so cool.

I hope you have a good time isolating.

Autumn and summer, especially winter.

I'm so sad this is my last letter to you. Hope you have a nice week and enjoy *Beyblade* episodes 27 and 28. Tell me your favourite part of episode 28. Hope you enjoy *Beyblade* every episode.

See you next week, Friday.

Harrison

*Letter 8 - Claire to Harrison*

Hi Harrison,

Thank you for your letter. I really enjoyed reading it. This is my last letter to you which is a bit sad. But it's been so fun writing letters for the past few weeks I think. Hopefully you will have another pen pal in the future. Like I said, I have had pen pals in the past and it's nice to receive letters. I particularly like getting letters in the post. And you can have pen pals from all over the world which is exciting.

I am sitting writing this letter in a coffee shop and Nelly is with me eating a chew. I have taken a photo of her. She is wearing her jumper now that it's a bit cold.

Sorry to hear you weren't very well last week. My isolation time is over now thankfully. It was OK, a little bit boring I suppose but as it's getting colder. Now I don't mind being indoors as much. Wow - that's good that you like winter. Do you like the snow? I just don't really like being cold.

I will keep watching *Beyblade* when it comes out on Fridays. I hope you are happy with the new ones that come out. It's good that they come out all of the time!

Anyway, that is all my news from this week. Thank you for taking the time to write to me over the past few weeks. I hope you have a great half term and get to do lots of fun things.

Speak soon,

Claire (and Nelly)

# Josh & Francis

*Letter 1 - Josh to Francis*

Hi, my name is Josh and I love to play football and play with my friends. I play for Celtic and I have been playing football for 11 years and I support Hearts.

I love chicken and pasta, and I really hate cheese (apart from on pizza). I also really like hotdogs as well. My favourite TV show is *Family Guy* and *The Simpsons*, and my favourite movies are *Ready Player One* and *Spider-Man: Into The Spider-Verse*.

I also like school and my favourite subject is P.E. and I absolutely hate French. I have three sisters. Their ages are four, 17 and 22. I don't really like them because they are all really annoying.

When I get home from school, I watch Netflix or go out with my friends. My favourite place is Barcelona because I love the football team, I have been there four times. I would love to go back to Florida to go to Disney World and see my family.

*Letter 2 - Francis to Josh*

Hi Josh,

Great to meet you!

My name is Francis. I'm married to Angie, and have two kids. Nancy is 19 and off to Uni in a couple of weeks. Tom is 17 and in S6 at school.

I loved your letter; it really made me smile. You've got great taste in films. I loved *Ready Player One* and *Spider-Man: Into the Spider-Verse*. I always used to read Spider-Man comics when I was younger, and I think he is still my favourite superhero. The book of *Ready Player One* is great too - it's quite long, but has detail they couldn't fit into the film. There's a sequel too *Ready Player Two*. Hopefully they will make that into a movie too.

I think Tom and Nancy can annoy each other, like your sisters. The thing they love doing together is watching *Rick and Morty* - any chance your sisters would watch it with you?

Sounds like you are a great footballer. I used to love playing, but was never much good. I'm from Sheffield originally, so I support Sheffield Wednesday. We're not doing so well at the moment - relegated to League One last year. Did you visit Camp Nou when you were in Barcelona? I've been to the city a couple of times but never visited the stadium. Is Messi your favourite player?

I'm running out of space, so I'd better stop here!

Looking forward to hearing from you soon.

Francis

---

*Letter 3 - Josh to Francis*

Hi Francis,

Great to receive your letter!

I have been trying to get a copy of *Ready Player One* but I cannot find it anywhere. I wonder if the book is the same as the movie, if it is then I would surely love it. Spider-Man is my favourite superhero as well and I'm looking forward to the new Spider-Man movie to come out. I am also really excited to watch this season of *Rick and Morty*.

I also think my sisters are annoying, especially my youngest one. She just started primary school a couple of weeks ago, but no, my sister probably wouldn't watch it with me. I play football three times a week and a game on Saturday or Sundays. Did you ever play for a football team or did you just play it for fun?

I have a great-grandad who was from Portsmouth and Nottingham. I am not sure if that is that close to Sheffield or not. Nottingham aren't doing too good at the moment either, they only have one point from six games.

What do you do for a living? Do you like what you do and what do you do in your spare time?

I have been to three Barcelona games; one in 2011 and another two in 2016, and yes, Messi is my favourite player ever and it's a shame he went to PSG. Barcelona aren't doing too good just now. I just don't think they are the team they used to be.

Looking forward to your next letter!

Josh

---

*Letter 4 - Francis to Josh*

Hi Josh,

Thanks for your letter, great to hear your news. You asked me loads of questions, so let me try and answer them!

I mainly played football for fun. I played for my school at junior school but wasn't good enough at senior school. I also played for a team at university and played in Sri Lanka when I lived there. I wasn't that good, so I mainly played hockey. The game awareness from football really helps with hockey. Have you played hockey at all?

Portsmouth is a long way from Sheffield. Portsmouth is on the south coast, but Nottingham is close, less than an hour away. Nottingham were quite big rivals for Sheffield Wednesday (when we were doing well!).

For work I do a job called 'Organisation Development'. It means I do the hiring for our company, and train people to keep their skills up to date. We have to think a lot about how people start work and have good careers. I like it, because I get to help people have a good career and a good life!

My biggest hobbies are cycling and running. I've run about 12 marathons, and some ultra-marathons. I once ran the whole of Hadrian's Wall in one day! As I get older my knees aren't so good, so cycling is better. I love being able to cycle for 50 or 60 miles as you see so, so much!

That's so cool about seeing Barcelona play. They're having a tough time now! Where would you like to travel to next? And what is your school like now? Does COVID make it difficult?

Do let me know. I can't wait for your letter!

Francis

---

*Letter 5 - Josh to Francis*

Hi Francis,

It's great to receive another letter! How has your week been? It's a shame that you didn't get into the senior team. I have played hockey a couple of times but that was in school for P.E. I liked doing it, but I found it hard that you could only use one side of the stick, and it did hurt my back a little bit.

I have never heard of an Organisation Developer but it sounds pretty cool! What's the most exciting part of your job? And what's your day like when you're working? I also love to cycle. I have a bike and a cycling machine in my house. I cycle when I go out with my friends and I sometimes cycle on my own. And I use my cycling machine when I don't go out or it's too cold! I used to go out for 5K runs to get fitter—I never used to like them but I had to do it anyway.

I am excited for this weekend because I can play my first football game in six weeks. I am hoping to play well and maybe score a couple of goals. I am playing against Hamilton.

Yeah, Barcelona aren't doing so well. I think they definitely need a better striker and better defenders. They are just not the team they used to be. I am looking forward to going to Turkey next year for two weeks and I got to pick where we went so that's the place I would love to go to. School is good with COVID, but the masks are very annoying and I think we don't need to wear them after October.

I am coming to the end now. I am looking forward to your next letter.

Josh

---

*Letter 6 - Francis to Josh*

Hi Josh,

Thanks for your letter, it was great to hear from you. How was your football match at the weekend? I hope it went well and you were able to score. I saw Messi scored against Manchester City earlier in the week. Even if he's left Barcelona, it is good to see him doing well.

We've had an eventful week - our dog has been really ill. He had to go to the animal hospital for six nights and they didn't know what was wrong with him. He is a black Labrador, and only six years old, so he is normally full of energy. Fortunately he is a lot better and he's home now. It was so strange when he wasn't here as he's so affectionate!

That's impressive about running 5K. It's a hard distance because you can run fast. As the distance gets longer you slow more and more, so it doesn't hurt as much! I bet you're having to use the cycling machine at the moment - it's suddenly raining a lot isn't it!

I hope you have a great holiday in Turkey - hopefully loads of sunshine. We've not got a holiday planned for a while, although my son and I are going skiing in February. He's a good skier, much better than me! We're going to Norway, which is a really nice country.

It's been great doing this with you - really enjoyed it!

All the best, Francis

---

*Letter 7 - Josh to Francis*

Hi Francis,

Thanks for your letter again!

My match went well. We won 4-3. Unfortunately, I didn't score but I did get an assist though. I thought I played well! I did see the game and Messi scored a brilliant goal. It's sad to see Barcelona beaten 3-0 again.

I'm sorry about your dog and I hope he gets better and fully recovers. I know how it feels because my dog sadly passed three months ago. He was 11 and he was a golden Labrador. He was like my best friend and I had had him since I was two years old.

When I did my 5Ks, I did it as fast as I could but my legs were aching after them. I think my top time was 25 minutes. I have been using my cycling machine more since it has started raining.

I hope Turkey is hot when I go as well because I haven't been on holiday in two years so I hope I hit the jackpot with the weather. I hope you enjoy your holiday as well. I want to go to Norway but I think it will be too cold for me. I would also like to do skiing but I would be useless at it though.

It has been really good writing these letters to you as well!

All the best to you and your family.

Josh

*Letter 8 - Francis to Josh*

Hi Josh,

I'm really glad you won the football match. Great to get an assist and hopefully you'll be scoring next time. Have you got games every week now?

Ralph (our dog) is much, much better now. We were really worried for a while, but he's back to his old self. He's got a lot of patches where the vet had to shave him, but thankfully it is all growing back quickly. I'm really sorry to hear about your dog. That's so tough, especially as you had him your whole life. I think Labradors are the best, the most friendly dogs there are, but ours is a black lab, so I'm a bit biased!

And 25 minutes is impressive for a 5K - I'm not surprised your legs were aching, that's a big effort. I think I'm going to have to use our cycling machine like you - with the rain it's not much fun being out on the road. When it is windy it is tough too - sometimes if you're cycling into a headwind it feels like you're not moving at all.

Have a fantastic time in Turkey. I'm envious of you getting some warm weather!

I've really enjoyed being pen pals. Hope you can carry on writing - my son who is in S6 now loves creative writing. He's written all sorts of stuff.

Best wishes to you and your family,

Francis

15/09/21

# Hi Louisa,

How are you? It was great to get your note telling me a bit about what you like. Wow, you are pretty busy! I am so interested to know more about the roller derby. How did you get together with your team? Do you have to wear a special kit?

I am really pleased to be paired up with someone who likes drawing (cute tomato!) as that is one of the most important things in my life. I know what you mean about not showing it to people, it always feels very personal... A part of my work is as an artist/illustrator so I have kinda got used to having some of my work on show but I always like to keep some things private, too. I agree about comics - I really like graphic novels too. Beautiful, detailed drawings or rough, crazy ones are equally brilliant. I just love to see people's ideas on the page. What are you doing in art at school right now? I would also like to visit Japan but I don't know how I would get there as I hate flying. ➤

# Louisa & Catherine

*Letter 1 - Louisa to Catherine*

My name is Louisa and I'm 13.

I like drawing (I don't really like showing people my art, I mainly do it when I'm bored).

I play roller derby, I'm part of a junior team.

I do diving (I'm not very good at it as I just started after not doing it for four years).

I'm a Guide.

I like comics and watching animation.

If I could go anywhere I guess I would go to Japan and I would want to see the cherry blossoms. I haven't been anywhere that far away before, or Egypt/Cairo as I would want to see the pyramids and go scuba diving.

*Letter 2 - Catherine to Louisa*

Hi Louisa,

How are you?

It was great to get your note telling me a bit about what you like. Wow, you are pretty busy! I am so interested to know more about the roller derby. How did you get together with your team? Do you have to wear a special kit?

I am really pleased to be paired up with someone who likes drawing as that is one of the most important things in my life. I know what you mean about not showing it to people; it always feels very personal. A part of my work is as an artist / illustrator so I have kinda got used to having my work on show but I always like to keep some things private too. I agree about comics - I really like graphic novels too. Beautiful detailed drawings or rough, crazy ones are equally brilliant. I just love to see people's ideas on the page.

What are you doing at school right now?

I would like to be able to visit Japan but I don't know how I would get there as I hate flying. Train would suit me pretty well. I love travelling by train.

Hey, maybe we should do a drawing every letter. I know you said you don't like showing your work but you have already achieved a public tomato.

Here is a seahorse for you

Anyway, looking forward to the project and to finding out your news!

Cheerio for now -
Catherine
P.S. Hope you can read my writing!!

*Letter 3 - Louisa to Catherine*

To Catherine,

I am good thanks. You asked about my roller derby. I first started by going to roller discos then the company that did the disco started trying to look for a team. My mom signed me up. We do have to have kit for it. We need knee pads, elbow pads, hand guards, a mouth guard, roller skates (obviously) and a team shirt. I don't like our team logo. I did submit a design for it but they mushed all our ideas together. On the shirt we also have our number and derby name on it. My number is 01 and my name is Tornado.

If you're an illustrator does that mean you have illustrated books. If so, which ones?

Doesn't it take forever to get to Japan by train? I'm fine flying by plane. The only countries I have been to are in Europe except Algeria.

How long have you been drawing for and what got you into it?

From Louisa

*Letter 4 - Catherine to Louisa*

Hi Louisa,

Thank you for your great letter. Wow, the strip you wear has a lot of different parts! You have really made me want to ask a lot of questions about roller derby - I've never met someone who's done it before. (For starters, why is it called roller derby?) I'm also guessing it must be a great spectator sport. Do your friends and family come and watch you? I'm also thinking that all the protective equipment you wear means you have to guard against injury. Hope you have managed to avoid that so far.

I love looking at book illustrations, but that's not my main thing. I do lots of pictures of people's houses, and the last weird job was to draw an event tent full of people to show how a festival would still be fun despite COVID restrictions. Also murals and workshops, sometimes online workshops. That is a whole thing that has taken off since COVID. I have always loved drawing - but now I love talking with other people about their drawing too!

Hope you have a great week - not long till the October break I guess - have you any plans?

Cheerio for now,

Catherine

*Letter 5 - Louisa to Catherine*

To Catherine,

My mom sometimes comes to watch my roller derby classes but the last time I played a game up against another team was before COVID when we went to Glasgow to play against another one of their teams. I haven't gotten injured in a game before though.

I don't always like sharing my art with other people but when I was younger I used to post art on social media. It was nice getting support from other people my age who like art. I don't really like art classes because I mainly draw as a hobby and don't like being told what to draw.

I also think this is meant to be my last letter.

From Louisa

*Letter 6 - Catherine to Louisa*

# Hi Louisa...

Glad you have avoided injury so far...!

Well, as this is the last time I'll be writing to you, I'm signing off - with big thanks for your brilliant letters. It's been great to have a window into your life and you have taught me a lot about Roller Derby!

I hope you keep drawing as well. I totally understand what you are saying about not always wanting to show people, but even as a secret hobby you just never know when it will give you something you can't get from anywhere else.

I hope you have a great year and thanks again for being a fab pen pal!

Cheerio for now,

Catherine

Hello Ryan
My name is Jo and I really enjoyed reading about how much you love sports, video games and football in particular. I'd be interested to know what you love about playing for your club St Johnstone FC and who your favourite Hibs players are and also what kind of video games you like.

I live very close to the Hibs stadium and when there is a big crowd the chanting and cheering is very loud!! I haven't been to a match — despite living so close — are there any games coming up that you are really looking forward to?

I share your love of pasta, tomato and basil and also of Barcelona. I have been fortunate enough to have visited the city twice. Also a friend of mine moved there to be a software engineer for Skyscanner, so I'll have to plan to visit him :). Did you travel there with your family? Did you learn to speak any Spanish words while you were there?

A bit about me: I grew up in New Zealand. I love cycling, camping, hill walking, gardening and drawing. I've played loads of sports over my many years, including: touch rugby, rowing, gymnastics, waterpolo and roller derby (it's like rugby but on roller skates!). I changed careers from graphic design to massage therapy to spend more time with people and less time on computers!

Looking forward to getting your reply. Take care.

...ore (I had to look it up too) was interrupted by Covid. It's been hard to adjust life around a global pandemic. We just have to do the things we can do and be kind to each other.
Looking forward to the next letter! Jo

# Ryan & Jo

*Letter 1 - Ryan to Jo*

My name is Ryan. For fun I play football and play video games. As you know I play football, I play for St Johnstone FC.
My favourite food is pasta, tomato and basil.
I support Hibs (Hibernian Football Club).
My favourite subject is P.E. because I love to play sports all day long.
My family. I live with my mum, dad and brother.
My favourite TV show/series is *Still Game*.
My favourite place in the world is Barcelona because it's such a nice place to go to.

*Letter 2 - Jo to Ryan*

Hello Ryan,

My name is Jo and I really enjoyed reading about how much you love sports, video games and football in particular. I'd be interested to know what you love about playing for your club St Johnstone FC and who your favourite Hibs players are and also what kind of video games you like.

I live very close to the Hibs stadium and when there is a big crowd the chanting and cheering is very loud!! I haven't been to a match – despite living so close – are there any games coming up that you are really looking forward to?

I share your love of pasta, tomato and basil and also of Barcelona. I have

Hello Jo

I really enjoy reading you letter, lot's of intersting things about what you love to do. So what I love about playing for St Johnstone is the long drives, night time games under the lights and love travelling. My favourite hibs Players are Macey the goilekeeper because I'm a goile, boyd because his pace is so fast and I love Jack Ross the manger.

My favourite video games are fifa, (I'm getting the new one)!! F1 the racing game. Yeah I travelled with my family and I have been to ~~fortun~~ fortunfenbra (sorr I can't really spell), it's such a nice place to go too. I didn't learn any spanish when I was over there, I was meant to go to Lanzarotta but because of COVID I can't go any more. :"

So you know I like to play video games but I'm never really in the house because I have training a lot Jo it's really hard to stay awake some times. 😊 zzz

I really enjoyed reading about what sports you like. I like hill walking as well, when I went I slipt and really hurt my shine and I was miles away from the car.

Can't wait for your reply.
From Ryan.

been fortunate enough to have visited the city twice. Also a friend of mine moved there to be a software engineer for Skyscanner, so I'll have to plan to visit him :). Did you travel there with your family? Did you learn to speak any Spanish words while you were there?

A bit about me: I grew up in New Zealand. I love cycling, camping, hill walking, gardening and drawing. I've played loads of sports over my many years, including: touch rugby, rowing, gymnastics, waterpolo and roller derby (it's like rugby but on roller skates!). I changed careers from graphic design to massage therapy to spend more time with people and less time on computers!

Looking forward to getting your reply. Take care.

---

*Letter 3 - Ryan to Jo*

Hello Jo,

I really enjoy reading your letter, lots of interesting things about what you love to do. So what I love about playing for St Johnstone is the long drives, night-time games under the lights and I love travelling. My favourite Hibs players are Macy the goalkeeper because I'm a goalie, Boyd because his pace is so fast, and I love Jack Ross the manager.

My favourite video games are *FIFA*. I'm getting the new one 😀 F1 the racing game. Yeah, I travelled with my family and I have been to Barcelona. It's such a nice place to go to. I didn't learn any Spanish when I was over there. I was meant to go to Lanzarote but because of COVID I can't go anymore. 😟

So, you know I like to play video games but I'm never really in the house because I have training a lot so it's really hard to stay awake sometimes. 😴

I really enjoyed reading about what sports you like. I like hill walking as well. When I went, I slipped and really hurt my shin and I was miles from the car.

Can't wait for your reply.

From Ryan

---

*Letter 4 - Jo to Ryan*

Ryan,

Thank you for your letter. It's wonderful to read about your dedication to your football club-they are lucky to have you.

Sounds like you sacrifice a lot to play for them and that is very admirable. Do you play and train all year round or is there a break over winter months? You said you play goalkeeper—I also think that is a great position→you might not get all the glory but you certainly have plenty of responsibility! Do you get to try different roles sometimes too? defence, midfield, attack?

I have to admit: I had to look up the video game you mentioned, *Titan*. Is it also known as *Titanfall*? It looks like a really smooth version of *Doom* (a game I used to play years ago :) ). I hope you get more of a chance to play the new version when you get it.

I'm sorry to hear that you got injured on that hill walk you did. It sounds like you had to suffer for a while to get off the hill with a sore shin. I am pretty lucky that I've never been injured even though I've climbed plenty of hills in Scotland. I climbed a few in NZ too, and they are even higher over there! I love the views you get from the top and there's always snacks and hot tea (that I have to carry up) as a reward.

Also, sorry to hear that the plan to travel with your family to Lanzarote (I had to look it up) was interrupted by COVID. It's been hard to adjust life around a global pandemic. We just have to do the things we can do and be kind to each other.

Looking forward to the next letter!

Jo

*Letter 5 - Ryan to Jo*

Jo,

I loved reading your letter, how has your week been? We play and train all year but when summer comes we take like four or five weeks off. When winter comes we take time off - the 21st November to the 5th Jan. I don't get to play in different positions but I don't mind not playing in different positions because I love playing in goal.

The hill I climbed when I injured myself is like 970 feet, so pretty big. I'm going to look up the game *Doom* that you used to play and I have to say it sounds really fun and cool to play.

Yeah, I do sacrifice a lot I guess but it's worth it because I want to make it pro one day so that's why I sacrifice a lot.

My favourite goalkeeper is David De Gea.

Have a good week (next week) :) Ryan.

Would you rather have hands for feet or feet for hands?

*Letter 6 - Jo to Ryan*

Ryan,

I've had a good week - thank you! One of the highlights was picking elderberries from my local park and making delicious balsamic vinegar. YUM! I made loads so I could share it with my friends but I might just keep it all!!! :)

I laughed a lot when I read your last question: hands for feet or feet for hands! It's got to be hands for feet - so useful - would you wear shoes or gloves on the feet-hands???! I imagine feet for hands would be super useful in goalkeeping!?

I read about David de Gea who seems to be the best goalkeeper around.

Not a bad role model to have when you want to be a pro! I wonder how much training he did when he was your age? I bet it was a bit easier to train for most of the winter in Spain - but in Scotland it can be baltic! How do you do it??!!!

Does your brother play football too? Do you have friends at Broughton who also play for St Johnstone FC?

I have a question for you: would you rather fight a horse-sized duck - OR - 20 duck-sized horses???

Have a good weekend!

Jo

---

*Letter 7 - Ryan to Jo*

Jo,

I had a good weekend. Feet for hands in goalkeeping would be pretty hard because if you had to catch the ball it wouldn't work! Because your toes wouldn't be long enough so it would be super hard.

David de Gea is the best in the world right now. He was playing on Tuesday night and he played amazingly! His team (Man U), would have lost but he kept his team in it. So training in Spain in the winter would be pretty good, probably like 20 degrees, so good but too hot for Scotland! I was training last night, (Thursday) and it was really cold! I just do it by putting more stuff on. At school none of my friends play for my team but they play for Hibs and Hearts.

My brother used to play football but he had a neck injury and then he was out but then he got replaced but now he has started to play golf.

I would rather fight 20 duck-sized horses because they would be small. :)

Would you rather have to wear goalie gloves for the rest of your life or have a floor of nails for the rest of your life?

Have a good week.

Ryan

P.S. This is my last letter so see you soon. Looking forward to seeing your last letter!

---

*Letter 8 - Jo to Ryan*

Ryan,

What a shame this is the last letter! I've really enjoyed our wee exchange and learning all about the world of football, video games and your life.

It's got really cold all of a sudden - like winter jumped in and declared "I'm here!". I hope you have plenty of gear to keep warm during training. Once again, I admire your determination when it must be so tempting to stay indoors and play *FIFA* instead. You can do anything you want to with that level of commitment!!!!

It's a shame your brother got injured and replaced. 🙁 A neck injury sounds awful. Trying other sports sounds like a good way to make the best out of a bad situation. I'm really glad I tried so many sports when I was at school. Some of them I only did for a year or two but it's never wasting time if you are enjoying yourself and making friends!

Hmmm...that's a tough one: goalie gloves or floor of nails from now on... I reckon I could learn to brush my teeth with goalie gloves but I don't think my feet would ever stop bleeding, so I choose the gloves.

Fingers crossed that the weather stays good enough to have an outdoor meetup later on, but in case I don't get to meet you: thanks for being a super awesome pen pal and stay cool.

Bye for now,

Jo

Dear Amerdeep

I hope your day is going good to, I'm having an ok day, today at school in hft we made stovies which is a scottish dish. It was super good.

I have tried the high jump and im really good at it! Im 13.
My favourite clothes shops are pretty little thing, shein and H and m.

All my sisters stay with me and sometimes we get along.

What annoys me the most is this boy in my class, he annoys both me and my best friend ayana.

I havnel been on the train recently but I am maybe going to on Sunday to my friend house since we have the day off.

Where are you from?
How old are you?
Whats your favourite food?
What is your favourite animal?
What do you do for a living?

From shefaly

# Shefaly & Amerdeep

*Letter 1 - Shefaly to Amerdeep*

Hi my name is Shefaly.

I like *Outer Banks* and my favourite subject is P.E.

I like being organised and being clean and smelling good and getting dressed up and looking good.

I like helping my friend with birthday parties and stuff and I love buying clothes.

I have three sisters. My favourite scent is Victoria's Secret Love Spell.

I am a middle child and I love Pepsi.

I want to live in Dubai and swim with dolphins.

*Letter 2 - Amerdeep to Shefaly*

Hello Shefaly,

My name is Amerdeep.

I hope that you are having a good day so far. How has your day been?

I am so excited about writing to you and to find out more about you. How old are you?

I see that your favourite subject is P.E. That is really good as exercise keeps you fit and healthy. What do you like doing in P.E.? I didn't like the high jump! I always used to knock the bar over. Have you tried it?

I see that you like to be organised. That is so good! You seem very organised.

I see you like shopping! What are your favourite clothes shops?

I also have three sisters. I love them very much. What things do you do with your sisters? Do they live with you? Two of my sisters live in London and one of them lives at home with my mum and dad. They are all older and have jobs.

What annoys you most? I find waking up early in the morning annoying!

I see you want to live in Dubai. That's amazing! It seems very warm there. Have you been?

I took the train to Edinburgh today for my job. Have you been on the train recently?

Speak soon!

Amerdeep 😀

---

## Letter 3 - *Shefaly to Amerdeep*

Dear Amerdeep,

I hope your day is going good too. I'm having an ok day. Today at school in HFT we had to make stovies which is a Scottish dish. It was super good.

I have tried the high jump and I'm really good at it! I'm 13.

My favourite clothes shops are Pretty Little Thing, Shiseido and H&M.

All my sisters stay with me and sometimes we get along.

What annoys me most is this boy in my class. He annoys both me and my best friend Ayusma.

I haven't been on the train recently but I am maybe going to on Sunday to my friend's house since we have the day off.

Where are you from?

How old are you?

What is your favourite food?

What is your favourite animal?

What do you do for a living?

From Shefaly

---

*Letter 4 -Amerdeep to Shefaly*

Hi Shefaly,

I have never tried stovies. They sound tasty. How do you make them?

That's amazing that you're good at the high jump! I wish I was!

I am good. How are you? I am busy at my job. I am a lawyer. I help people with problems they have.

I am from a place called Bathgate. I don't know if you have heard of it?

I am 33 years old. Very old!

My favourite food is pizza. You?

I used to be scared of dogs but now I love them! You? Do you have any pets?

I hope that boy is not annoying you a lot. Have you told your teacher?

Speak to you soon!

Amerdeep

*Letter 5 - Shefaly to Amerdeep*

Hi Amerdeep,

Stovies are good! To make them you just cook beef with onions and then add in water with potatoes and you cook it then you're done.

I'm good, too, and yes I've heard of Bathgate.

My favourite food is pizza as well but also chicken wings. Pizza toppings - Jalapeno and chicken.

I like dogs but sometimes they are scary! I have two big fish tanks with fish in them. I also have three hamsters and two guinea pigs. I share them with my sister.

I am having a maths test on Tuesday and Thursday. I'm also having a science test on Monday and I've already had my history test.

I watch this show called *Outer Banks* and my favourite character is SS. You should watch it. It's very adventurous and mysterious.

Speak soon, Shefaly

I'm very good at singing, my friend said.

From Shefaly

*Letter 6 - Amerdeep to Shefaly*

Hi Shefaly,

I hope that you're having a good day!

You're so good at cooking! I am so bad! I would burn them!

I love jalapeños! They are so spicy but nice!

Good luck on your tests. My advice would be to stay calm, read the question carefully (at least twice) and don't panic! You will be great. :)

You sound like you love animals!

Good luck in the rest of school. Always remember that you can do anything. Don't be scared to dream big. Sometimes you feel scared and that is OK. You can be anything you want. People used to say to me that I was not brainy enough or loud enough to become a lawyer. I ignored them and I am a lawyer now. You can be anything you want! Be happy and work hard.

Take care and lots of love,

Amerdeep

---

*Letter 7 - Shefaly to Amerdeep*

Dear Amerdeep, hello,

I love Jalapenos too but I don't find them spicy and I really like spicy food.

I got an A in my science test and an A in my history test. I already did my maths test but I'm waiting for my maths test mark.

I love singing and I want to be a plastic surgeon when I'm older though.

I can't wait for Halloween. My costume is so cute. I'm dressing up as a person with a mask and matching with my friend.

I'm sad this is our last letter. It was fun writing to you! I'm excited to meet you and I will tell you how I got on with my maths test.

From Shefaly xxx

*Letter 8 - Amerdeep to Shefaly*

Hi Shefaly,

This is our last letter! I feel a bit sad as it has been so enjoyable speaking to you and I cannot wait to meet you in person.

You did very well in your tests! You should be so proud of yourself! Good luck in your maths results. I am sure you will have done great!

Plastic surgeon! That's amazing! Remember you can be anything if you work hard and have faith in yourself.

Have fun at Halloween. Your costume sounds really fun. I have a little girl aged three and we are going out trick-or-treating. 😁

Look forward to meeting you soon!

Amerdeep

PART TWO

# YOU'VE GOT MAIL

## THE PEN PALS OF MS ANDERSON'S CLASS

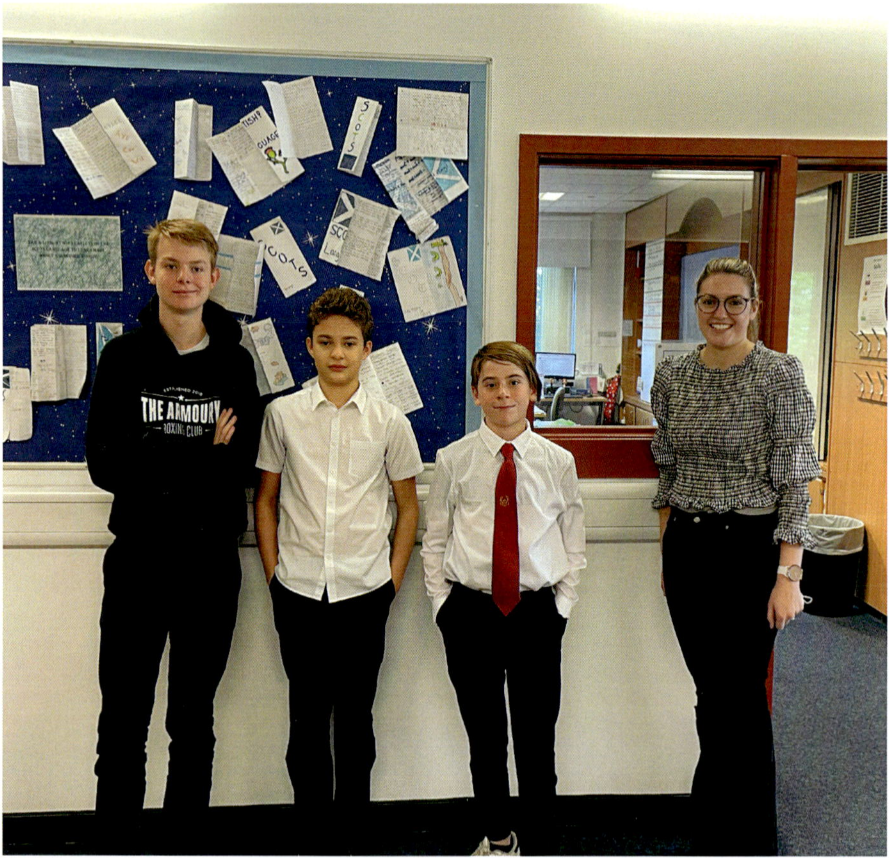
SCOTS
SCOTS
THE ARMOURY
BOXING CLUB

# Introduction

≈ ABIGAIL ≈

To think pen pals could make so many people so excited! Classmates who seemed to carry a strong dislike towards writing were eager to receive their next letter. You couldn't expect to connect so strongly with people you've never met, you don't know anything about, but still bring such enjoyment while communicating with them.

When Gerald and Jessica first came into 2X5, the reactions varied from uncertainty to curiosity. Some weren't sure how to begin, while others filled over a page the first time we wrote our letters. Gerald and Jessica were an amazing help with starting and were a huge amusement in the eight weeks they stayed with us, thinking of ways to keep us engaged. I watched my friends' faces light up when they remembered the Super Power Agency would be coming in again week after week.

Just after everyone received their first letter, many couldn't wait for the next. The letters were filled with such joy. I spent time learning about France and many other random topics from my pen pal, Valerie. Max was shocked at the amount of similarities between him and his pen pal. Ivan burst with joy as he rambled on about video games in his letters. We were writing to people with large families, the old, the young, people who were different, people who were new.

Thank you to every one who made this possible, Gerald and Jessica - the organisers of the Pen Pal project, our teachers, every one of my classmates and especially the volunteers who helped make it possible. And thanks to you for picking up this book and reading to hopefully learn something new like we all did. Who knows what will come next?

Abigail from Ms Anderson's class.

# Abigail & Valerie

*Letter 1 - Abigail to Valerie*

Hi, I am Abigail K and I enjoy a variety of things. I play the guitar, violin (well...still learning) and I sing. I watch anime though I can't decide on a favourite. I love the book *Anne from Green Gables* and I enjoy writing. It's my way to express my emotions. I love autumn because of the gorgeous colours and the general vibe. My favourite weather is a thunderstorm because it makes amazing sounds. The raindrops against any surface is my favourite sound.

I don't have a favourite subject as I like most of them, but maybe science is my favourite just now, although that changes a lot.

*Letter 2 - Valerie to Abigail*

Hi Abigail,

Great to get your letter and to know a little bit about you. I haven't had a pen pal for a long time. It's really fun writing to someone who lives in the same city, but you might otherwise never meet.

I'm Valerie. I live with my husband, three children and two mini dachshunds (sausage dogs). We recently moved back to Edinburgh after living in Paris for nearly four years, so we're just getting to know the city again. Do you have any brothers and sisters, or pets? Have you lived anywhere else? Would you like to stay in Edinburgh or travel when you're older?

One of my son's is really into anime. He has lots of books about it and watches it on TV. I like the way the characters are drawn and that the stories tell you a lot about life in Japan. My youngest son loves Pokemon and can tell you all about their evolutions. I think there's a shop near Waverley station which sells lots of Japanese stuff, so we might have to visit that. Have you ever played *Pokemon Go*? It was a big thing in Paris but not so many people seem to have it on their phones here.

It's great that you're so musical. Do you think that's something you'd like to make into a career or is it just a hobby? I learned guitar at school but it made my fingers hurt trying to get the right notes so I gave that up. I like singing too. Are you in a choir? Are there any other instruments you'd like to learn to play? What sort of music do you like?

This morning there were leaves on the ground so autumn is definitely on it's way. I love the cold, clear days and how the trees change colour. It always feels like the start of the countdown to Christmas and I've already seen Christmas sweets in the shops - eek! Do you get an October holiday from school?

*Anne of Green Gables* is a fantastic book. What are you reading now? I can see you're already a great writer and they say that everyone has at least one story in them, so maybe you'll be an author one day. I work with lots of writers and authors and they're using social media to get everyone reading again because lots of people seem to have forgotten how good it is to curl up in a cosy place with a new story. I recently read *If Cats Disappeared From The World* by Genki Kawamura. It was first written in Japanese and has now been translated into lots of different languages. It's about the meaning of life and is enjoyable for all ages, you might want to look out for it. What other books would you recommend?

I don't think I had a favourite subject when I was at school either, but I was better at things like English, languages and chemistry than I was at maths. There is so much you can learn online now. Did you do online school during COVID? Do you prefer actual school?

Thanks for taking part in the Super Power workshop and really looking forward to your next letter.

Valerie

---

*Letter 3 - Abigail to Valerie*

Dear Valerie,

What was Paris like? I would love to visit Paris one day. I have a younger sister and we get along well. In terms of pets I used to have a hamster called 'Chilly' but she died. She was an amazing hamster so it's not a pain to think/write/talk about it anymore.

Does your son have a favourite anime? I love to see the art style change every time, every new series, and then try to redraw the characters. I think anime shows many aspects of life and I enjoy trying to figure out what happens next. What do you enjoy watching generally?

Pokemon used to be a huge thing in the past, and I played it a little but not much. Now people still play but as you said, it's not extremely popular these days.

I think music will continue to be a hobby for me. I really enjoy it but I would prefer to do something else, for example, an author or something to do with psychology. Maybe a neurologist or a chemist. What do you do for work?

I'm currently reading the second part of *Twilight*, the first book of *His Dark Materials*, *Sophie's World* and I'm planning to read *Dune* and *Eragon*. If you say it's a good book, I'll add *If Cats Disappeared From The World*. Also remembered that *Red Queen* is also a series I'm reading.

I find that I enjoy speaking to someone online and somehow always manage to ask them to recommend a book.

What are you currently reading? Have you read anything else I mentioned? Have you ever visited any other country?

I strongly disliked online school so I'm very happy we're back again. How did your family deal with COVID?

I am terrified of animals, but I love them at the same time. I would like a Border Collie in the future. What are the names of your dogs? Do you have any fears?

I am really jumping around the place with this letter so I'll just carry on like that. I'm not part of a choir but I am a Girl Guide. I would love to learn to play the flute. Do you have a favourite song? Mine is *Devil Town* by Cavetown but it changes a lot.

It was amazing learning about you and I look forward to learning more. Awaiting the next letter!

Abigail

---

*Letter 4 - Valerie to Abigail*

Hi Abigail,

It was really exciting to get your letter. I feel like I should be sending you a handwritten reply rather than an email, but I'd hate for it to get lost in the post, so this is probably safest. Paris was an adventure for our family. I did Higher French and my boys had done a little at school, but other than that we all had to learn the language as we went along. There are lots of differences between Paris and Edinburgh, but they are both beautiful old cities. Even though we've been back for almost a year, we still eat croissants for breakfast on the weekends and listen to French music like Bigflo & Oli. Ask me anything about Paris living and I'll try to answer.

Sorry to hear about your hamster. They do make good pets, though, and Chilly is a cute name. I had two hamsters when I was growing up. One called Henry, who was always escaping, and one called Dolly, who was a long-haired grey hamster. My middle son had pet rats when we lived in France. It sounds weird, but they were gentle and clean and really fun to have around. Do you think you'll get another hamster?

My son likes all kinds of anime. He has some *Attack on Titan* books and some *Dragon Ball Z*. The artwork is amazing, but I find the stories a bit complicated to follow because you have to remember who all the characters are.

I used to work for big corporate companies like Adobe (who make computer software), but when my first son was born I decided to set up my own company helping businesses with their marketing. Facebook launched the same year, so I got really interested in social media, and now I spend a lot of time advising on how companies can use social media to reach their customers. It's funny that this wasn't even a job when I was at school. It sounds like you're interested in all the right subjects to be ready for the future. What would your ideal job be? Would you stay in Scotland or move abroad?

It's great that you read so much. I'm going to look up all those titles you mentioned. I read lots as part of my job, but for fun I've read the *Miss Peregrine's Peculiar Children* series. Have you read them or maybe seen the film?

I've been lucky enough to travel all over the world and would definitely recommend it if you get the chance. It's hard to pick favourite countries, but Japan and Iceland are first to come to mind. Have you been abroad? Where did you go? Where would you go if you could go anywhere? Whenever I'm on a trip I try to see one of the animals that you can only find there. I think seeing animals in the wild would really help you get over your fears. I'm claustrophobic, which is a fear of small spaces, so I'm not keen on finding native animals if they live in underground burrows. Do you have a favourite animal?

My dogs are called Walnut (he's brown) and Raisin (he's black). Walnut is 10 and Raisin is eight months, but they seem to get along, although the puppy is much faster than the pensioner when we go for walks. Border Collies need lots of exercise, but they are also super smart and easy to train. I hope you get one someday. It's great to have a wishlist for the future. Perhaps by the time you're my age there will be cyber pets, or at least robotic versions of what we have today. Have you seen videos of artificial intelligence dogs?

Top work on being a Girl Guide. I was in the Girls Brigade when I was younger and my sons were in Scouts when we lived in France. It's great being a member of something outside of school. What's your favourite thing to do at Guides? Do you have many badges? Have you had to camp out?

Thanks for introducing me to Cavetown. I hadn't heard of that band before, but I like their music now. There's a band called the Indigo Girls that sound quite similar, so maybe you can listen to some of their stuff. I'd love some more recommendations for new music. What should I listen to next?

Hope you're having a great week. Write back soon!

Valerie

*Letter 5 - Abigail to Valerie*

Hello Valerie,

Your letter was great! I prefer it written digitally because I'm honestly horrible at reading handwriting, though I've heard your handwriting can say a lot about you.

Paris seems interesting. I love the language and I plan to take it in school. Do you have a favourite word in French? I listen to some French music once in a while (but nothing specific because I love how it sounds). Did you live close to the centre? How would you describe the view from the Eiffel Tower, if you've been there?

My friends used to have some rats. They were more acquaintances than friends. They would seriously abuse the rats, but they died before we got to do anything cause they ate chocolate. It was really sad. I hope the rats are OK, wherever they are.

I don't think I'll get another hamster. At least not any time soon. I remember once Chilly made a hole in the corner of her cage and my parents had to screw on a bit of metal. It was safe, though.

I've never heard of the *Miss Peregrine's Peculiar Children* series, but I'll have to add it to my reading list!

Could you explain more of how your job works? I'm not much into that topic, but I want to know more, please?

I DO NOT want any AI creatures in my house. Those things sound terrifying. I'll check out that band though, and glad you like Cavetown. Other artists I like include Alex Benjamin, Tally Hall, and Mother Mother!

My favourite animals are WOLVES! They're amazing and amazing and cute and fierce and AMAZING! What is your favourite animal?

Farewell then!

Abigail

---

*Letter 6 - Valerie to Abigail*

Hello again, Abigail.

I loved your last letter. Wolves in capital letters made me laugh. You really like them a lot, huh? Supposedly there were wolves in Scotland until the end of the 18th century, and I've read that there is a project going on in Sutherland to reintroduce them to the wild in the next five years. Fingers crossed. I've always loved penguins and whales. While I've been lucky enough to see whales several times, penguins are still on my wish list. I've had to content myself with those in Edinburgh Zoo. Have you ever seen the penguin parade there?

Your handwriting is so neat. I'm sure if someone were to analyse it they'd think you were very organised and creative. I can't believe we're nearly at the end of the Pen Pals Project, though. I feel like we're just getting started. Has this been a fun workshop for your class? I've really enjoyed getting to virtually know you and it's great to think there are letters and emails flying around between people who live in the same city but who otherwise might never meet.

If you like French music you should give Zaz a listen (or a watch on YouTube). She's a singer-songwriter who mixes jazz, soul, and acoustic. I think you'd like her. We lived about 15 minutes from the Arc de Triomphe, and an easy walk from the Eiffel Tower. Paris is laid out on a grid, with very wide streets and ornate buildings. You should definitely go there, especially at night when the city sparkles. There is also a less well-known tower called Montparnasse, which has equally great views of the city and the added bonus that you can actually see the Eiffel Tower from there. You might like to watch a film called *Midnight in Paris*, which is a romantic comedy about time travel, but also shows you lots of the city. If you had a time machine where would you go? Would you be tempted to drop in on your future self? What do you think you'll be doing 10 years from now?

My job involves lots of writing. Sometimes it's blog posts or captions for social media, but I also help businesses know what they should do to market (which really just means sell) their products. I've worked with lots of interesting companies and people, including Scottish Ballet and The Edinburgh Fringe Festival. No two days are ever the same and I love working from home, so I can still take my dogs out and walk my youngest child to and from school. I think the important things with jobs is to find something you really love to do and then it doesn't feel like work ; )

Are you looking forward to the October school holidays? Will you go away or stay in Edinburgh? We're going to London to live in a house boat for a few days. I normally get sea-sick, but it should be fine since we won't be moving. Have you ever been on a boat? Hope you're a better sailor than me.

Do you have a favourite food? My family all love anything spicy. Do you cook? If so, what do you like to make? I prefer baking to cooking.

I mostly make banana bread and chocolate chip cookies. Did you watch *The Great British Bake-Off*? Do you do any classes around food at school?

I guess I should leave you time to write a reply. Thanks for the other music recommendations, too – they're great and have helped me to seem more up to date with my children, who often roll their eyes at my musical tastes.

Hope you're having a brilliant week at school.

Valerie

---

*Letter 7 - Abigail to Valerie*

Hi Valerie,

It's honestly insane that this project is ending soon. I just got told there is a possibility we might meet and I'm a bit astounded. It is just a possibility, though. It has been a fun project! It's really weird talking to someone like this who I don't really know. You mentioned before that you had other pen pals before. Were they from before you left for Paris?

Glad you found the wolf business funny. I love spending my time watching documentaries about them. I am kind of scared of the wolf project in Scotland but I would love that. Is it a good idea, though? I do not know.

I've been to Edinburgh Zoo, but never for the penguin parade. What types of whales did you see? I believe you'll find a way to see wild penguins, one way or another.

I've never actually listened to soul music. Do you like it? I listened to Indigo Girls and they sound extremely cool. I adore that style of music. I don't currently have any new recommendations. The songs/groups I mentioned before aren't very popular artists, but still are names you'll hear about the place. I've been listening to a lot of classical music lately. Can't memorise any names, though.

I'm not much of a holiday person. But this time I'm hyper excited because I'm going to a Guide camp. It was cancelled at first because of COVID, but because the restrictions are falling, we're allowed to go finally. It's meant to be so much fun!

I have never been on a big boat, only canoes. Do you like any sports? I like everything to some extent, but I don't DO any as a hobby. I don't have a favourite food. I can survive spicy stuff. I won't complain if I have to eat it, but I'm not a huge fan. All of my friends love spicy food, though. Banana bread is a big thing now, I'm not sure why. I tried to bake it once. It was fine. I don't bake loads, though, so probably lack experience.

At school we have a subject called HFT (health and food technology) where we get to cook once in a while. School had been terribly calm until now. We had no homework before but because the end of term is incoming, we have a lot of assignments and tests. But it's all going well.

What was your favourite business to work with? Do you ever play any games or are you too busy? Any TV programmes you watch?

I missed a whole paragraph. If I could move to a time period I'd go to the past, like late 1800s. I wouldn't want to see myself in 10 years, because I prefer not to know than see something bad. What about you?

I'll search up the movie and Montparnasse. Why is the Eiffel so popular then? You haven't told me your favourite word in French and I'm really curious about that.

I have to go now cause I'm out of time. This was very amazing and fun. Hope to meet you one day. Awaiting a reply!

Abigail

*Letter 8 - Valerie to Abigail*

Hi Abigail,

I've heard there's a plan for us to meet in person, too – that would be fabulous! It has been so good writing to a total stranger and week by week getting to know a little more about you. I'll miss your letters! I have to admit that every time I pass your school I wonder if you're one of the people I can see. Oh, and my whole family are now hooked on Tally Hall, so without knowing it, you've made a positive lasting impression on us.

My previous pen pals have always been around my own age and have tended to be people I've already met on holiday or through other friends and then we decided to stay in touch. This project works because it mixes people who might otherwise never meet and shows them they've got a lot more in common than they'd first think. There's a brilliant video on the Super Power Agency website showing what happened when a previous class wrote to a group of people who were probably ages with their grandparents. Have you seen it?

There's still lots of debate about reintroducing wolves to Scotland. I think it might be like *Jurassic Park* (have you seen that film?), where everyone starts out being amazed and then get slowly more frightened as the animals stop being controllable. The current idea is to put the wolves in a fenced-off area of about 200 miles at the most northerly tip of Scotland, so we probably wouldn't have to worry about escapes. But as Jeff Goldblum says in *Jurassic Park*, "Life finds a way". As an aside, did you know that Jeff Goldblum is an amazing jazz pianist? I saw him in concert in a tiny theatre at the foot of the Sacre Coeur (a popular landmark and the second most visited site in Paris after the Eiffel Tower, which is the most popular because it's so big and easy to take photos of, I guess).

Speaking of France, there are lots of great French words. Here are a few:

Cerf-volant = kite (but it literally translates as "flying deer")

Un froid de canard = freezing cold (but it translates as "a cold for ducks")

Pamplemousse = grapefruit (and is just fun to say)

Top news re: Guide camp. You'll have soooooooo much fun. Are you staying in tents? Do you get a special badge for attending? I'm so glad the restrictions are lifting to let this go ahead. There's something really special about being away with a group of friends at a camp like this, and I'm sure you'll have loads of happy memories as a result. Maybe you'll go back as a leader one day? Are they still called Brown Owls? Which badge do you most want to get?

I wasn't really into sport while I was at school, but I loved dancing – tap, ballroom, Latin American, and basically everything you see on *Strictly*. I went to lots of competitions and my gran used to keep all my medals and trophies in a big display case in her living room. Now that I think about that, I should ask my mum where they all went – ha ha.

Re: games and TV, I used to play *Zoo Tycoon* and *Mario Kart* with my children. I'm told there's now a Mario Land in Universal Studios theme park in Japan, so that you actually feel like you're in the game. I'm not sure I'll ever run a zoo though ;) We've been watching the *Stranger Things* series because I hear that season 4 will be coming out soon. Before that, it was mostly Marvel movies. (Did I mention my children are all boys?!)

When it comes to time travel, I think you're right that it's best not to visit yourself in the future, just in case you don't like what you see. I would like to go back in time, though. Imagine if you could clarify some of the mysteries of the world, like what colour dinosaurs were or whether there ever was a city of Atlantis?

My current favourite business to work with is the Super Power Agency. Gerald, Claire, and the team do an amazing job and they're always full of ideas for new projects (like this one). They're also great listeners, so if you have any suggestions for future workshops they'd love to hear them.

I've suddenly realised that I'm asking you all these questions, but you won't get a chance to reply. Fingers crossed that we get to meet, or I'll never know.

It has been an absolute pleasure to write to you, Abigail. Your letters have been smart and funny and beautifully written. I hope the rest of the school year goes well and best of luck for the future. (I just know you'll do great things!)

Valerie

Dear Adrianna,

Hello, I am very excited to ha[ve]
a penpal and to getting to know [you]
letter.

...love.
You say you would like to go to Hawaii,
an island surrou[nded by] sea, with lots
of beautiful col[ourful fish?] ...and Disney
Island. The Is[le of ...]
Isle in the I[sle of ...]
...Ki[ngdom]...

I collect stamps. Which is your favourite on this page and why?
Need to find some for Hawaii ♡

3.
Art? I like to paint and love
making things with shells from the beach.
So many questions, but here are
a few....
When is your birthday and have you
always lived in Edinburgh?
I like cooking as it is creative.
What do you like to cook and what
is the most delicious thing you like
to eat? I love cheese scones!
I hope you have a really good
week at school and I am very
excited to hear from you soon.

Best Wishes Maxine

What is your favourite colour? Mi[ne is]
Blue. It represents the sea whic[h]

# Adrianna & Maxine

*Letter 1 - Adrianna to Maxine*

My name is Adriana C.

For fun I like to read, talk to friends and watch Minecraft streamers. I like to watch anime and Disney movies, but the anime has to have either love or hate in it.

My favourite food is everything.

My favourite subjects are English, art and ICT. In English, I like to read. In art I get to be creative. In ICT I like to do computing.

I would like to visit Hawaii.

*Letter 2 - Maxine to Adrianna*

Dear Adrianna,

Hello, I am very excited to have a pen pal and to get to know you by letter.

I see you like anime and Disney movies. Which is your favorite Disney movie? I have started watching anime as I have not really seen very many. Thank you for the top tip, they are so good.

You like Art and Design. Minecraft is very creative. I am a designer and I love creating. I like designing houses and love to use colour. What is your favourite colour? Mine is blue. It represents the sea which I love.

You say you would like to go to Hawaii, an island surrounded by sea, with lots of beautiful colours. I come from an island. The Isle of Man. It is an isle in the Irish Sea. Part of the United Kingdom. We would be very cold if we wore grass skirts though like they do in Hawaii! If you are from the Isle of Man you are called "Manx". The Isle of Man is known for cats with no tails, called Manx cats.

Do you have a pet? What is your favourite animal? What is your best thing to do in art? I like to paint and love making things with shells from the beach.

So many questions, but here are a few: When is your birthday? And have you always lived in Edinburgh?

I like cooking because it is creative. What do you like to cook and what is the most delicious thing you like to eat? I love cheese scones!

I hope you have a really good week at school and I am very excited to hear from you soon.

Best wishes,

Maxine

P.S. I collect stamps. Which is your favourite on this page and why? I need to find some for Hawaii.

---

*Letter 3 - Adrianna to Maxine*

Dear Maxine,

Hi, I am very excited to get to know you. My favourite Disney films are *Lion King* and *Raya* and *the Last Dragon*.

I recommend watching *Your Name* on Netflix. When you start watching anime, it's better to start with little kids' anime like *My Neighbour Totoro* and *Spirited Away*. It's really cool that you are a house designer. My favourite colour is blue.

I have a pet dog and her name is Bella. My favourite animal is a red panda. My favourite thing to do in art is drawing animals and making fortune tellers.

My birthday is on the 20th of May.

I have lived in Edinburgh from 2015 to now. So that is six years, maybe seven.

I like to bake cookies. My favourite thing to eat is chocolate.

I would like to ask some questions. What age are you? What anime have you seen so far? Did you watch any Disney movies when you grew up?

My favourite stamp is the Queen of Scots one.

From, Adrianna

---

## Letter 4 - *Maxine to Adrianna*

Dear Adrianna,

Thank you so much for your beautifully written letter. Your handwriting is very good. I love that we both love BLUE. So many amazing shades. Which is your favourite? I think I like them all!

My birthday is June 1966. That makes me much older than you! The anime I watched was *A Silent Voice*. I really liked the way the characters are designed. My favourite Disney movies from my childhood were *Snow White* and *101 Dalmations*. I still love watching them now!

What kind of dog is Bella? Do you bake her cookies?

I will watch *Your Name* today, as I think you have good taste in films.

Please draw some animals or a *Minecraft* animal. What is a fortune teller? That sounds so interesting.

I have two dogs. Orri (who is a Parson Jack Russell) and Toro (who is a black Labrador Retriever). They are good friends, but Orri can be a bit naughty!

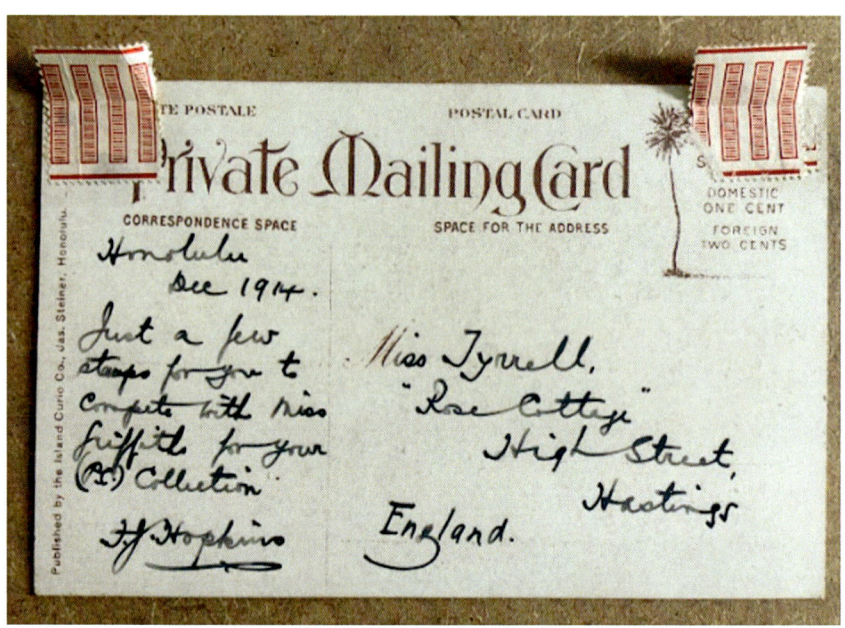

Honolulu
Dec 1914.

Just a few stamps for you to complete with Miss Griffiths for your (X) Collection

J.J. Hopkins

Miss Tyrrell,
"Rose Cottage"
High Street,
Hastings
England.

---

I like to visit vintage, charity and Antique shops. I found this postcard from 1914 from Honolulu Hawaii. I thought you would like it. Do you like to collect anything.

20th September 2021
EDINBURGH

Dear Adrianna,

Thank you so much for your beautifully written letter. Your handwriting is very good. I love that we both love BLUE. So many amazing shades. Which is your favourite? I think I like them all!

My birthday is June 4th 1966. That makes me much older than you! The anime I watched was 'A SILENT VOICE'. I really liked the way the characters are designed. My favourite Disney movie from my childhood was 'SNOW WHITE' and 1001 Dalmatians. I still love watching them now!

What kind of dog is Bella? Do you bake her cookies?

I have lived in Edinburgh for 10 years. Before that, I have lived in London, New York, and the Isle of Man. Where did you live before Edinburgh?

My favourite music band is Fleetwood Mac and my favourite Scottish singer is Callum Beattie. What is your favourite music to listen to?

Look forward to hearing from you again.

Bye bye for now,

Maxine

*I like to visit vintage, charity, and antique shops. I found this postcard from 1914 from Honolulu, Hawaii. I thought you would like it. Do you like to collect anything?

---

*Letter 5 - Adrianna to Maxine*

Dear Maxine,

Thank you for the postcard. It is lovely and my favourite shades are ultramarine blue, sapphire blue and violet blue.

My birthday is May 2008. I saw a silent movie. It was interesting. Bella is a Jack Russell mini.

I used to live in Poland in a little city, and my favourite music to listen to is Bruno Mars.

I am sorry for the short letter. I am doing this on a computer.

---

*Letter 6 - Maxine to Adrianna*

Dear Adriana,

Thank you for your letter. Lovely to hear what blues you like, and that Bella is a Jack Russell. Although they are small dogs, they have BIG personalities. I bet she is Queen Bella in your house!

Since thinking about all the blues we love, I am noticing them more everywhere, everyday! I enjoy making a collage which is a kind of art. It is a colourful way to make art and you can use old magazines and newspapers. I made you a blue collage on the cover of this card. Perhaps you can try to make one yourself.

Silent movies are interesting to watch. I loved watching *The Artist*. It is about a silent movie star and there is a little dog in it.
I think you will like it a lot.

I hope to hear from you again if you have time, doesn't matter if it is short as you are doing lots of other things too like lessons.

Bye bye for now,

Maxine

---

*Letter 7 - Adrianna to Maxine*

Dear Maxine,

Is so sad that this is the last letter I will write to you. How are you doing and feeling? Bella is a little princess. Bella hates rain. When it rains, she will lay on the sofa and sleep. She has learned to bark.

Collages are fun to do. I did some collages at home, but it is all about *Minecraft*. It is so nice of you to make a collage for me. I will watch *The Artist* and I will enjoy it, and you can watch *word fazz up*. It's amazing.

I had a test; I got an A. I am proud of myself.

I hope to hear from you again for the last time.

Bye,

Adrianna

*Letter 8 - Maxine to Adrianna*

Dear Adrianna,

Thank you for your letter. I loved hearing about Princess Bella!
I completely understand about the rain. Maybe we should make her a raincoat for her walks!

For my last letter, I wanted to show you one of my favourite artists. The late, great FRIDA KAHLO. Her portrait is on the cover of this card. She had a very unique style and loved colour. She lived in a bright blue house with orange window frames and green doors. So cool and very stylish for her time.

It is sad this is our last letter, but I just wanted to say how much I have enjoyed writing to you. Also, to tell you that being creative and loving art has made my life much richer, so keep up your art and when you get more great grades, remember I am clapping and willing you to do more lovely work.

Keep working hard, keep up your writing. It is beautiful and keep smiling in a BLUE colourful world.

My best wishes.

Good luck,

Maxine

# Angus & Alastair

*Letter 1 - Angus to Alastair*

I like to play video games, read books and watch TV. The sports I like are football, American football, field hockey and swimming. I like watching action, comedy, and mystery. The shows I have watched include *Scorpion*, *Brooklyn Nine-Nine* and *The Simpsons*. My favourite foods include fast food, pasta, Mexican food and Japanese food. My favourite subject is HFT because I enjoy cooking and being creative. A lot of my family are musicians or work with the NHS. I like music and I play the saxophone. I would really like to visit New York City.

*2 - Alastair to Angus*

Dear Angus,

Hi! I'm really pleased to be writing to you as part of the Pen Pal project. I got your introduction and I'm impressed – it sounds like you do a lot!

A quick introduction: my name is Alastair, I live in Leith with my family and a cat named Maudie, who is a bit fat and always complaining that she hasn't been fed.

I'm a computer programmer and a children's author, which is a strange combination of things to do, but I enjoy it. I like nice food, books, TV and films and computer games, and music, but I can't play an instrument AT ALL.

This is Maudie, wanting fed (again).

I'm not into a lot of sports, although I like watching rugby. I've been to a few Scotland games, but usually when I go they lose, and if I stay at home they do better :-). Did you see Emma Raducanu winning the tennis US Open? I thought she was amazing. I can't believe she's only 18! When I was 18 I thought getting out of bed was an achievement :-). Do you like playing sports as well as watching?

I like TV programmes – I also like *The Simpsons*, and I've seen a few episodes of *Brooklyn Nine-Nine*. My youngest daughter LOVES it – I think she knows the lines off by heart. I haven't seen *Scorpion*, but it sounds pretty good. We've been watching *Ghosts* recently – that's the one that's got all the actors from *Horrible Histories* in it. It's very silly, but lots of fun. I love films, too, especially Marvel films, but I'm a bit out of date – I haven't seen *Black Widow* yet, or *Shang-Chi*, have you? I'm looking forward to the next James Bond movie! If you like mysteries and comedies, you might like *Knives Out* – it's a murder mystery film, and really good fun.

I love Mexican food (especially fajitas), and pizza, and sushi – actually, pretty much anything. What's your favourite? I see you like Japanese food, is there a restaurant you like going to? We went to Yo Sushi not long ago, and it was awesome. I'm impressed that you enjoy cooking – I can't cook at all, I'm terrible at it! What kind of cooking do you like best? Is there something you're especially good at? My dad was a chef, so when I was growing up I used to get lots of really nice meals :-) My parents managed a hotel, and then owned a restaurant. I hated doing waitering, so I would work in the kitchen washing dishes. It was hot work! Do you think you'd like to be a chef?

I saw in your introduction that you wanted to go to New York one day. I'm very lucky – I've been there twice! I got to see the Statue of Liberty and the Empire State Building, I saw the New Jersey Devils play, and I ate sushi at a very fancy place where the chef cut the pieces of fish up and tossed them straight onto our plates. It was a very cool place to visit :-) What would you see first if you went there?

Looking forward to your first letter.

Cheers, Alastair

---

*Letter 3 - Angus to Alastair*

Hi Alastair,

Thank you for the first letter, it was really nice. I have been to a lot of Scotland rugby games as well. I did not see Emma Raducanu because I don't like tennis (except when Andy Murray is playing). Do you support a football club? I support Manchester United because of my grandma. I have two guinea pigs. I like grumpy cat. I would like a cat but my family are allergic to them. I am also learning guitar.

I really like all kinds of food, but I don't like sandwiches and lasagna (which is weird because my favourite food is spaghetti bolognese). I have seen *Black Widow* and *Knives Out*. I like to cook anything and everything I can eat. I think I would like to be a chef. I have been to New York and I have seen the New York Knicks play at Madison Square Garden.

From, Angus :)

---

*Letter 4 - Alastair to Angus*

Hi Angus!

It was good to get your second letter, thank you. I hope you've had a nice week? My weekend has been very busy – in fact, I spent most of today making props!

They're for a show I'm taking part in next Saturday, to do with a book I wrote called *INCH and GRUB*. It's a picture book for young children, about two silly cavemen who squabble about who has the best stuff.

The pictures aren't by me (I'm terrible at drawing!), but by an artist called David Roberts.

The book has been out for a few months now, and next weekend I'm going along to the Wigtown Book Festival to do a storytelling session and a show. It's very exciting to be able to do 'real' shows again with a real audience, instead of Zoom calls and virtual events! But I'm a bit nervous, too. 😂

I know what you mean about the tennis. I'm like you, I only ever watched when Andy Murray was playing. But I happened to be watching the TV when the US Open finals came on, and I thought, why not? It was a really exciting game! I was interested in you saying you support Man U because of your Grandma. What's the story there? Is she a big fan? Have you been to any home matches?

I don't really have a football team I support. I don't know much about football, but I grew up in Perthshire, so when people asked, I always used to say St Johnstone. And since nobody cared about St Johnstone, that was fine. But then they started doing really well, and winning cups, and suddenly people have started asking me what I think about the players – and then I have to admit I don't have a clue! It's well embarrassing. 😂

It's a shame about your family being allergic to cats but if you have two guinea pigs then it might be for the best – they might not like having a cat around! My oldest daughter had two hamsters, one called Pickle and one called Cucumber. There's only Pickle left. If you'd like to find out what happened to Cucumber then let me know but be warned: it is a GRUESOME TALE OF HORROR....

I think it's great that you'd like to be a chef. Like I said, my dad was a chef, and my brother-in-law is a chef, as well. We love going to their house because we always get brilliant food! It's very hard work, but very rewarding, I think. Do you cook a lot at home? What's your best dish? My dad wasn't much of a football fan, either, but one time he got invited to a match by the chef who did the VIP food for Dunfermline Athletic. Neither of us had any idea about the game, but we loved being in the Private Members lounge. You got special tiny posh Scotch pies. 🥟🥟🥟

Cheers,

Alastair

P.S. It's very cool that you got to go to New York and see the Knicks!

P.P.S. Sorry that this letter is typed, not written like yours. I do a lot of typing, but hardly any handwriting, and over the years my writing has become terrible. Even I can't read it! It looks like worms having a fight. ☹️

---

*Letter 5 - Angus to Alastair*

Hi Alastair,

Thanks for the letter. It was my birthday on Monday. I got an ice cream maker, a Spider-Man game for PS4, and a paddleboard! That's what I was most looking forward to. I have only been paddleboarding once at Loch Morlich in the Highlands, but I really enjoyed it so I got a dry bag which you put on the front of the board and it keeps them dry. I have not used it yet but I think I will today.

I went to my favourite restaurant. It is called Five Guys. Have you been?

You also said in your first letter that you like video games. What games do you play?

I play the saxophone and as I was taking it out the reed (the bit of wood that you blow on) had mould on it. Yuck! I'm so glad I didn't put it in my mouth.

I support Man United because my gran is from there. For my ninth birthday I went to get a tour of the stadium. I saw the changing rooms, I walked down the tunnel and saw the pitch!

I am intrigued to find out what happened to Cucumber.

Also, do you have a console? I have a PS4.

Cheers

Angus :)

---

*Letter 6 - Alastair to Angus*

Hi Angus!

## HAPPY BIRTHDAY!!!

Hope you had a good day – it sounds like you did! I've never tried paddleboarding, but I've always wanted to, so that sounds like an awesome present. And an ice cream maker! Brilliant. Have you tried it out yet?

And yes, I've been to Five Guys, and I really like it. It's my youngest daughter's favourite place, she's always raving about it. She likes the bacon cheeseburger. 😌

I don't have a console, and mostly I play games on my phone. But I have to be careful – I get obsessed with them and stop getting anything else done. So after a while I have to uninstall the ones I really like. 🙁 I've been playing Slay the Spire a bit – it's a pretty simple game where you have to make it to the top of a tower, fighting bad guys. You fight by playing cards, so you have to collect different cards and build up your deck. I like those kinds of games, where you have to think about your move. I played a bit of Fortnite, but my older daughter kept beating me all the time, and then laughing at me. ☹️

It's very cool that you got to go to see Old Trafford! But yuck, disgusting about the mould on your saxophone reed. My eldest daughter used to play the trombone, and the most disgusting thing I ever saw was her emptying the spit valve. YUCK. She plays the piano now – there's a lot less spit. ☺️

(Actually, these days she plays her own piano, because she's now away at university. She went up this year to St Andrews to study psychology. It's very strange to have just the three of us in the house now, though of course we all keep in touch and text and send photos and things.)

Now... Cucumber. if you're really sure you want to know... Here is THE SAD, TRAGIC, HORRIFIC TALE OF CUCUMBER THE HAMSTER. (Be warned – it's gruesome!)

Pickle and Cucumber were dwarf hamsters, and they belonged to Rose, my oldest daughter. We picked dwarf hamsters because they usually get along with others, and we thought they could play with each other and not get bored or lonely. And they did – they scurried around their little cage, chased each other, snuggled up next to each other when they slept, and Rose loved them both to bits.

Pickle seemed to be the boss, and maybe a bit of a bully. He would quite often run up and poke at Cucumber or push him out of the way of the food, or steal his bits of nest. But Cucumber never seemed to mind ...

... until one evening, Rose came upstairs looking upset. She was holding something in her hands, very carefully, and she said:

"Cucumber just attacked Pickle! I think Pickle's going to DIE!"

Poor Pickle was in a terrible state. He was covered in blood, one ear was half chewed off, and his back leg was hanging loose and looked broken. We don't know what had happened, but perhaps Pickle had just pushed Cucumber aside one too many times, and Cucumber had gone BERSERK. Cucumber had turned into a Red-Eyed Hamster Of Death.

Now, fortunately Pickle did survive. These days he only has half an ear on his left side, but otherwise he's OK and quite happy. But what could we do about Cucumber? They certainly couldn't live in the same cage anymore! We brought him upstairs and put him in my younger daughter's room, in an old spare cage, and decided they would have to live apart.

Cucumber didn't like this new cage. He was always scurrying over the bars and gnawing at the wire that held the door closed. But we had to keep him in there, because of our cat, Maudie. Maudie is a bit fat, and very lazy, but she does occasionally catch mice, so we had to keep Cucumber safe.

In fact, Maudie actually caught a mouse a few days later. We were in the living room when we heard her chasing it. There was a tiny, sad, squeak, and then a THUMP. When I went to investigate, there were the remains of a fat grey mouse, and Maudie looking pleased with herself.

Well, it's a bit grizzly, but I suppose that's what cats do. I put the poor wee dead thing into a bag and into the bin.

It was only later that we realised the truth. That evening, when my younger daughter Amelie went up to her room, she noticed that the cage door … was open.

"Cucumber's escaped!" she shouted. We all searched for him, but he was nowhere to be found. And suddenly, I had a terrible thought. I crept out to the bin and found the bag, with the poor dead mouse. And I realised it wasn't a fat grey mouse at all… It was a hamster.

We don't know exactly what happened. Somehow, Cucumber gnawed the wire loose and opened the cage door. Somehow, he climbed down from the table where the cage sat. Somehow, he made it down the stairs, though each stair was twice as tall as him. How did he do it? We don't know. Why did he do it? We don't know. Perhaps he just wanted to explore? Perhaps he wanted to make friends with Pickle again? Or perhaps, filled with murderous rage, he had set off to finish what he'd started…

Either way, when he finally made it downstairs, he discovered, not Pickle, but Maudie the Cat – who was very pleased to see him.

And that was the end of Cucumber. 😁

Cheers,

*Alstr*

---

*Letter 7 - Angus to Alastair*

Hello Alastair,

Thanks for the most recent letter. The story of Cucumber is very sad.

You said you were a children's author. What books have you written? I am currently reading *Percy Jackson and the Titan's Curse*. I really like reading. My favourite book series is probably *Harry Potter*. What's your favourite book?

I went paddleboarding twice on the weekend. The first time in the sea, but I started to drift off to sea and my mum told me I had to jump in the water so I didn't disappear. The second time was in a lake, but that was much better because there were no winds and I couldn't disappear.

I also played my first hockey game for my new club. The first match we won 2-1, and the second we won 6-0! I was very happy.

Thanks, Angus :)

*Letter 8 - Alastair to Angus*

Hi Angus!

Sorry for sending you such a horrible story about poor Cucumber the Hamster! It was a bit sad. :( But I like to think that Cucumber did get to have an adventure first. These days, Pickle is all recovered, and quite happy. My daughter, Rose, is away at university now, and Pickle couldn't go with her, so he stays here with us and we take turns looking after him. He loves exploring, but we don't let him get too close to Maudie the cat!

Yes, I am a children's author, although it's only been a few years now and it still seems weird to say it out loud. Actually, I have two jobs - for most of the week I'm a computer programmer, and then for the rest of the time I write books. I've got a few now!

I write picture books for very young children, and science fiction adventures for older readers, like you. And starting next year, I've got a whole series of books coming out about dragons, for younger readers. (I've only got one cover for that so far because the rest are still being finished!) I don't draw the pictures, because my drawing is so bad that it would make small children cry.

It's great fun being a children's author. I really like getting to do school trips and meeting classes. I haven't been able to do very much because of lockdown, but hopefully I can do some again soon.

I like the Percy Jackson books - I think it's a cool idea having gods and mythological creatures just wandering around and getting into trouble. :) My favourite book is one from when I was about your age, called *The Grey King*, by Susan Cooper.

It's a bit beaten up! That's because I read it about a thousand times. I read it until the cover fell off. I dropped it in the bath, twice, and had to dry it out with a hairdryer. I *loved* this book! It's about a boy who is part of a group of magicians, trying to save the world. But he's been ill and lost his memory, so he's trying to get better, but he knows there's something urgent he's supposed to be doing. It's part of a series called *The Dark is Rising* and it's probably the book that made me want to be an author.

I get to read a lot of books for kids, which is great, because I love them. I read *The Memory Thieves* by Darren Simpson, and that's really good, and *Tiger Skin Rug* by Joan Haig, and *Troofriend* by Kirsty Applebaum, and *Monstrous Devices* by Damien Love. There are a lot of brilliant books out there! Also, if you like Percy Jackson, you might like the *Skulduggery Pleasant* books by Derek Landy - they're exciting and really funny.

Your paddle boarding adventures sound fantastic! I think your mum must have been a bit nervous that you'd end up washed out to sea and land in Norway or something. :) A lake sounds like a better idea, for sure. Sounds like you're enjoying it though!

And it's good to hear about your hockey - 6-0! Blimey. It's great that you're getting a chance to play. I'm really looking forward to life getting back to normal.

So, I think this is the end of the Pen Pals project, but I wanted to say, thank you so much for your letters - I really enjoyed reading them, and I'm impressed at how much you get up to! Good luck with the new hockey team, and I hope you get to go back to New York soon!

Cheers,

*Alstir*

Edinburgh, 5th September 2021.

Hola Iván,

How're you? My name is Edvardo and I'm also Spanish. This is why I know that your name has a wee accent on top of the "a".

Where are you from? I am from Málaga but moved to Edinburgh in 2008. I also like chorizo but the food I miss the most is "pescaditos fritos", which is local small fish from Málaga deep fried.

I'm sorry that I'm not a big fan of videogames. However, my nephew Alex (10) loves "Minecraft" too. He lives in England, so I only see him a few times a year. I've asked him to teach me to play a couple of times, but I don't think he's very interested. It must be boring for him! How do you play "Minecraft" with or is this something you play by yourself?

I also like art although I don't do anything. During lockdown, I've missed museums (a lot!). I really enjoy going to photography exhibitions when there's one in Edinburgh. And I love the two Modern Art Galleries in Edinburgh.

The thing I like the most is reading. I have around 500 books, although I've not read all of them yet. My partner says that I should put some in the charity shop because we're running out of space.

I hope school is going well. Last year was hard for everyone and I'm sure you missed your friends.

Looking forward to hearing from you!   Edvardo

# Ivan & Eduardo

*Letter 1 - Ivan to Eduardo*

I am Ivan V.

I play video games and create digital art.

I like badminton.

I like *Stranger Things* and *Pokemon*.

I love pasta and chorizo.

My favourite subject is art because I like art.

I would love to go to Tokyo and visit lots of places there.

To me, video games are EVERYTHING.

My favourite video game is *Friday Night Funkin* because of its modes and hard difficulty.

*Minecraft's* good too, I like building houses and castles.

I am also Spanish.

I play piano and harp.

*Letter 2 - Eduardo to Ivan*

Hola Ivan,

How're you? My name is Eduardo and I'm also Spanish. This is why I know that your name has a wee accent on top of the "a".

Where are you from? I am from Malaga but moved to Edinburgh in 2008. I also like chorizo but the food I miss the most is "pescadito frito," which is local shellfish from Malaga, deep fried.

I'm sorry that I'm not a big fan of video games. However, my nephew Alex (10) loves *Minecraft* too. He lives in England so I only see him a few times a year. I've asked him to teach me to play a couple of times, but I don't think he's very interested. It must be boring for him! Who do you play *Minecraft* with or is this something you play by yourself?

I also like art although I don't do anything. During lockdown I've missed museums (a lot!). I really enjoy going to photography exhibitions when there's one in Edinburgh. And I love the two modern art galleries in Edinburgh.

The thing I like the most is reading. I have got so many books, although I've not read all of them yet. My partner says that I should put some in the charity shop because we're running out of space.

I hope school is going well. Last year was hard for everyone and I'm sure you missed your friends.

Looking forward to hearing from you!

Eduardo

*Letter 3 - Ivan to Eduardo*

Hola Eduardo,

Nice to meet you. I'm glad you like chorizo.

I am from Huelva. I moved in 2016 to Edinburgh and one of the foods I miss most is 'choco frito.'

I used to play *Minecraft* alone but some of my friends joined some of their friends and now we play *Minecraft* as a group of 10 in survival mode.

Reading is my passion, my favourite books series are *Diary of a Wimpy Kid* and *Harry Potter*. What are your favourite books?

One of my favourite topics is science and space. I don't know if you know this, but I want to be an astronaut. I'm fascinated by black holes and want to be one of the first people to set up a space station next to a black hole to study it.

I also play a rhythm game called *Friday Night Funkin* and I'm making my own modification to 'mod' the characters: Nauland Laifer.

Do you like memes? If so, could you tell me what type? I want to hear more from you and about your day-to-day.

Excited to talk more,

Ivan

---

*Letter 4 - Eduardo to Ivan*

Hola Ivan,

Thank you very much for your letter. I really enjoyed reading it!

I have to tell you something very funny. When I told my partner, Ben, that my pen pal's favourite food was "chico frito", he thought it was "fried chocolate." He's from England so I believe he was picturing a deep-fried Mars bar or something like that. By the way, have you ever tried deep-fried Mars? I never did. I think they look very revolting.

I've only read the first Harry Potter book and, I must admit, I find it a bit boring, so I didn't try the others. Some people have told me that the story gets much better after book two (from book three, I mean). What do you think? When I was around your age, in Spain, I used to read a series of Spanish books called *Manolito Gafotas*, about a boy with big glasses. They're very funny! There's also a film based on the book. I am sure that your parents have read them or at least they know the story. Do you read in Spanish or only in English? I tend to alternate between both languages.

Your idea of being an astronaut and exploring black holes sounds amazing and very inspiring. I love ambitious people! Do you have any steps prepared for this? Which subjects do you need to choose in high school to study astronomy at university? Because I guess that's what you need to do, but please correct me if I'm wrong. Have you ever been to the observatory in Blackford Hill? I've never been inside but I've walked around plenty of times. I love the views from there.

I'm pretty intrigued by your question about the memes I like. Maybe because I'm old (although not very old: I'm turning 40 in two months), I use memes and GIFs in a different way. I generally insert them in a conversation. For example, on WhatsApp or with one of my colleagues in the internal chat, instead of saying "thank you", I find the "GIF" of a famous person receiving an Oscar and saying "Thank you". By the way, what's the difference between a GIF and a meme? I use these two words interchangeably.

By the way, I don't think I've told you that I work as a content designer for the Scottish Government. A content designer is someone who writes things like web content or information on leaflets, etcetera. I like it, but my secret (or not very secret, since I'm telling you now) dream is to be a novelist one day. I love stories, which is why I began to volunteer for the Super Power Agency almost two years ago, but they've had to be paused because of COVID.

I hope you have a great week.

Looking forward to hearing from you,

Eduardo

P.S. You can call me "Edu" if you want to. Everybody in Spain calls me "Edu".

---

*Letter 5 - Ivan to Eduardo*

Hola Edu,

Thank you for your response. I have tried the Mars bar and it is OK. While writing this, something funny happened and you would understand it: A girl in front of me started saying a Spanish insult, so I asked her "What did you say?" and she looked at me and repeated the insult. I then said louder, "You know, that's really offensive". She then stared at me and said "Oh, right, you're Spanish". She then turned back to her desk and said, "I have one brain cell". I almost died of laughter.

The Harry Potter franchise does get better after the second book. My parents have read and seen *Manolito Gafotas* and have told me to read it, but I'm still thinking about it. I read both English and Spanish. Some of my *Diary of a Wimpy Kid* are in Spanish and others are in English.

I know how to be an astronaut; I just have to study physics and astrology. I have never been to an observatory.

GIFs and memes are almost the same. GIFs just move. It's very cool that you work for the Scottish Government. I would like to work as soon as possible in a fast food place to gain some money.

Excited to hear more from you.

Ivan

P.S. Just gonna draw my character cause I think he's cool.

*Letter 6 - Eduardo to Ivan*

Hola, Ivan.

How're you this week?

Thank you very much for your letter. As usual, I really enjoyed reading it!

Here's a small pressie for you: Greta Thunberg's book. I find her very inspiring and her message very important. I wish there'd have been someone like her when I was your age. Maybe we'd not have reached this point with the climate crisis. Who knows? If you have the book or you're not very interested, feel free to pass it on. I believe that books always find the right hands for them.

My job sounds better than it actually is, to be honest. I love the people, but sometimes it's a bit boring because I need to wait for the managers' instructions, and some of them are very busy. So sometimes I spend my day waiting for an email back, and other days are super busy, when all managers respond at once and I have loads to do!

Can you tell me more about your character? I tried creative writing in Madrid and there's an exercise to create a character's personality: describe it/them in five lines. For example: Harry Potter is 1) he has a scar on his forehead; 2) he's a magician; 3) he lost his parents when he was very young; 4) he's shy (sorry I'm not sure about this), and 5) he wears glasses. How's your character's personality/backstory? You told me their name is "Navi", right?

Looking forward to reading your next letter.

Eduardo

*Letter 7 - Ivan to Eduardo*

Hola Edu,

Thank you so much for the book. I was searching for something to read. I will read it as soon as possible.

Your job seems like high school to me – looked fun but it was very boring. But I see us working for the government as someone important.

Navi is an anthropomorphic goat who represents me in the online and cartoon worlds. It's based on a character from the game *Undertale* called Asriel. Navi was created by the devil as a weapon, but has no control over him. He was left in the old world for 19 years and was adopted by a family. He loves his sister and is very caring about her. There's also a character about his sister, called Laifer. She is a normal person and represents my sister. Laifer likes having Navi around because one day they were playing some games and Navi destroyed a table, so now she knows his power. Navi also transferred power to Laifer so she could defend herself against harm.

Thank you so much for your letters, it was very fun to talk to you.

Ivan

*Letter 8 - Eduardo to Ivan*

Hola Ivan,

Thank you very much for your letter! I really enjoyed reading it. Although I should clarify that not everyone who works for the government is someone important. I am not James Bond! :) I read the letter on the same day when I went to see the new film. It's very good!

Today is a funny day. Because it's my birthday in Edinburgh: I arrived in this city 13 years ago!!!

It's very interesting that you based your two characters on you and your sister. Do you think that J.K. Rowling drew Harry Potter on herself? That would be an interesting question. I guess you know that she lives in Edinburgh. I saw her once in a cafe where she was with some friends.

But what I mean is that I guess all writers take elements from their lives or those around them. That's one of the basic mottos I always heard: write about what you know.

I know this is our last letter. I want to tell you that I've really enjoyed it and I'm very hopeful about the future: this world is in safe hands if new generations are as cool as you are!

Take care!

Edu

Hi Adrian ♥

I did watch the Derby it was very exciting I was disappointed we never won but I enjoyed it do you watch football? if so what team do you like?

I have not tired martial arts and would like to have a go I'm not sure wich one do you have a suggestion?

I don't like gherkins or lettuce on my burger. I'm not very good at cooking but I do make a good cup of tea but thats about all.

I don't have a pipe I'm a bit young. I like how funny it is. I love comedy shows.

I really enjoy the Ancient Greeks it is very fascinating also WW2 and the Romans also the Vikings.

I know Ottowa and Quebec because I am good at geography and enjoy it do you enjoy geography?

I will hope to hear from you soon Adrian
best regards
Leon.

# Leon & Adrian

*Letter 1 - Leon to Adrian*

For fun I like to play my PlayStation 4 and enjoy playing football. I play for a football team and I support Hibernian Football Club. I also enjoy playing badminton and like basketball.

I like to watch *Still Game* and comedy shows. My favourite food is beef burgers.

I really enjoy history for learning about the past and the wars that happened.

I would love to visit Canada. It's just a beautiful place, particularly Ottawa and Quebec.

*Letter 2 - Adrian to Leon*

Hi Leon,

I have never had a pen pal before so this is very exciting! You mentioned in your bio about being a Hibs fan? I believe it was the derby match against Hearts last weekend? Did you watch it? What was the game like?

With you already doing football, badminton and basketball, it sounds like you enjoy trying out different sports? I used to play lots of rugby and started martial arts when I was 15. I still train and practise different types of martial arts whenever possible. I think I have had a go at almost all of them now. Is there a sport you haven't tried yet that you would like to have a go at?

I must admit I do like a good burger, especially with all the extra bits like lettuce, gherkins, mayo and chunky chips. I have become quite good at making my own at home now. How are you at cooking? What's your special dish?

*Still Game* is very funny but I would never have guessed that you would like a show about old people. Have you got a flat cap and a pipe? What do you like about the show?

It's great to hear that you like history, so do I! In my job I get to research lots of stories from the past and sometimes meet really interesting people. We are very fortunate to live in Edinburgh and be surrounded by so many museums, art galleries and ancient buildings. I especially enjoy finding out about the stories that some of the paintings show. What part of history have you found most interesting?

I have only visited Canada once, but you are right, it is a beautiful place and also the people are really friendly. I travelled to a small town called Yellowknife, in the very north of the country. It was minus 26 degrees most days and we got to go ice fishing and drive on an ice road - basically crossing a frozen lake as a shortcut between towns. They were even driving huge lorries across it! This was the place where they made the TV show *Ice Truckers*. It seems like lots of Canadians have relatives in Scotland, is that how you know about Ottawa and Quebec?

I am away fishing tomorrow and hopefully in my next letter I will be able to boast that I caught lots of fish. I look forward to hearing from you soon.

Best wishes, Adrian

*Letter 3 - Leon to Adrian*

Hi Adrian,

I did watch the derby. It was very exciting. I was disappointed we never won but I enjoyed it. Do you watch football? If so, what team do you like?

I have not tried martial arts and I would like to have a go. I'm not sure which one. Do you have a suggestion?

I don't like gherkins or lettuce on my burger. I'm not very good at cooking but I do make a good cup of tea but that's about all.

I don't have a pipe, I'm a bit young. I like how funny it is. I love comedy shows.

I really enjoy the Ancient Greeks. they are very fascinating. Also WW1 and the Romans. Also the Vikings.

I know Ottawa and Quebec because I am good at geography and enjoy it. Do you enjoy geography?

I will hope to hear from you soon, Adrian.

Best regards,

Leon

*Letter 4 - Adrian to Leon*

Hi Leon,

It is good to hear from you. Although the Pen Pal Project is officially over, I thought it only good manners that I reply, as you had taken the time to get back to me.

I was brought up in Liverpool and was a huge fan when I was in school. I collected all the posters, autographs, and transfer stickers. Unfortunately, I was a rubbish football player and much more suited to playing rugby. I don't watch football much now, more of a rugby fan, but I have friends who go to all the Hibs games and I have been to a Hibs versus Hearts derby match. They really don't like each other!

You were asking about which martial arts you might try out. There are so many different types and clubs across Edinburgh. I'd suggest checking out somewhere close to home, so you can train regularly. Most encourage you to come along first and watch a class and many also let you try out a couple of classes for free. Brazilian Jiu Jitsu (BJJ) is very popular at the moment, and also kickboxing. I started out doing karate and Judo, and now I do Kali, BJJ, Muay Thai, Kickboxing, and JKD. Check them out online and see if any of them appeal to you.

Good to hear that you are enjoying geography at school. I really liked it too, and have done lots of travelling. My first trip was when I was 17 and I travelled on my own by train across Europe to Turkey. It was quite scary at times, but also amazing to experience such a different culture and to see how different the architecture and food was. Since then, I've travelled a lot, until the COVID outbreak made us all stay home! Two of my favourite places that I plan to visit again soon are Samoa and Tonga in the South Pacific.

It has been nice to be a pen pal with you, Leon, and hopefully the Super Power Agency will run another project in your school very soon that you can take part in.

Have a great Halloween, Bonfire Night, and Christmas.

Best wishes,

Adrian

13.09.21

Dear Maximilian,

Thank you so much for your letter.
You sound so interesting and creative — art and design often go together. I'm very like you, I love art and have ~~~~ ~~~~ me, paintings and sculpture. I ~~~~ things work. My ~~~~ your f~~~~

I love "Starwars" too — I've seen them all. Who do you like best? Which droid is ~~~~ Who would you like to be ~~~~ film?
~~~~ but not snails either. ~~~~ school or do you

start your own company. Tesla are fantastic and Lego is a great way to develop creative and technical skills. Is Denmark where Lego was developed? It seems a great company. One of my children loved Lego technic. Have you been to the new lego store in the St. James Centre yet?

My father in law ran a big shipyard in Glasgow. His grandfather developed a boiler because he was supposed to be praying in church one day, and he looked at his hands and thought what a good design this would be for the pistons on a boiler!
The Yarrow Boiler was created from his idea!
Which Tesla would you buy if you could?

Praying hands.

# Maximillian & Sheila

*Letter 1 - Maximillian to Sheila*

My name is Maximilian F. I'm 13 years old and 6.1 feet tall. In my spare time I love to draw or read. I also love to play with my LEGO, play video games, play with my brother or just be lazy and watch TV. When I watch TV, I almost always (anytime no one is using it) watch *Star Wars*. I'm a massive *Star Wars* fan/nerd. I'm not kidding when I say that I enjoy literally everything about *Star Wars*, I even watch everything related to *Star Wars*. So let's just say I am a big *Star Wars* geek.

When it comes to food, my favourite dish is a steak or beef burger, but I hate snails.

When I grow up, I want to start my own car manufacturing company (like Tesla).

My favourite subject is art. I really love to draw and design so much it seems weird. I probably get it from my dad, who's a famous artist. My mum is great too, she's a model. Once she worked with The Queen and I got to meet her. I was five though so I don't remember it that well.

If I was to go somewhere it would be Denmark.

*Letter 2 - Sheila to Maximillian*

Dear Maximilian,

Thank you for your letter.

You sound so interesting and creative - art and design often go together. I'm very like you, I love art and have been selling some paintings and sculptures. I also love to find out how things work. My mum let me cut up a toothpaste tube when I was a kid, so we could see how the stripes got into it. Do you still get stripy toothpaste?

How old is your brother? I have two sons and six grandchildren.

My dad used to work with The Queen too as her press secretary. We got to meet her when we were teenagers. I am tall too and remember thinking how small she was!

I'm retired now but used to be a primary school teacher. I'm glad you want to start your own company. Tesla are fantastic and LEGO is a great way to develop creative and technical skills. Is Denmark where LEGO was developed? It seems like a great company. One of my children loved LEGO Technic. Have you been to the new LEGO store in the St James Centre yet?

My father-in-law ran a big shipyard in Glasgow. His grandfather developed a boiler because he was supposed to be praying in church one day, and he looked at his hands and thought what was a good design this would be for the pistons on a boiler! The Yarrow Boiler was created from his idea!

Which Tesla would you buy if you could?

I love *Star Wars* too - I've seen them all. Who do you like best? Which droid is your favorite? Who would you like to be if you were in the film?

I love most food but not snails either. Do you have lunch in school or do you go out?

Hope you have a good week.

Love, Sheila

P.S. What projects are you doing in art this term?

*Letter 3 - Maximillian to Sheila*

Dear Sheila,

You sound like an amazing person.

It's great that we have so much in common, it's almost mad. I saw how many questions you asked, which I love. Denmark is where LEGO was developed. It's an interesting story, actually, and I have been to the St James LEGO store. I think it's heaven. Stripey toothpaste is my favourite of all toothpastes.

My brother is 10 years old now, and still a menace. How old are your sons? Crazy that we both met The Queen and it's cool that your dad used to work with her. That queen has been around for some time.

Thank you for the support for starting my own company. Tesla are, for sure, fantastic. If I could, I would buy the Tesla Roadster. Do you have any other car companies that you like or hate? Your father-in-law sounds like a creative, nice guy. I would love to hear more about him.

*Star Wars* for the win!! I love Darth Vader, his backstory is amazing. My favorite droid is R2-D2, and if I wanted to be in the movie, I would be Luke Skywalker.

Loved your letter.

From, Max

---

*Letter 4 - Sheila to Maximillian*

Dear Max,

Thank you so much for your letter.

Are you going to see the new James Bond film? I love those films. My little grandson, Henry, is five, and he wants to watch *Star Wars*. Which film do you think we should show him first?

My son, Ross (who is 36), loves Teslas too, and got to drive one of the first Roadsters back in 2011, before the Model S went into production. Do you like SpaceX as well? (Elon Musk is CEO of both.) Did you see that the new Model S just set a record at Germany's famous Nürburgring race track for the fastest-ever electric vehicle, beating the Porsche Taycan, which previously had the record?

Could you draw a picture of your dream car? This could be your first design for getting funding for your company. Would it be electric, hybrid, or petrol?

It's great to have big dreams. The world needs people like you, Max!

Have a good weekend.

Best wishes,

Sheila

---

*Letter 5 - Maximillian to Sheila*

Dear Sheila,

I loved reading your letter.

Yes, I'm going to watch the new James Bond. My brother loves Bond, especially his DB5.

For Henry's *Star Wars* movie, I would start with *A New Hope* – the first one made. It was the first one I watched, as well. Your son, Ross, sounds really into cars, like me. I also love SpaceX. I followed them from the start. They're literally bringing us into the future.

Here is my car drawing:

It's called the Bennett Shark. It's fully electric, with a top speed of 200 mph.

It was fun talking to you. It's sad that it's over, but it's fun while it lasted.

From Max

Best wishes.

---

*Letter 6 - Sheila to Maximillian*

Dear Max,

I'm so impressed with your design of the Bennett Shark and love its spec. You're very talented - keep designing and inventing!

Thank you for your advice about *Star Wars*, too. Hopefully we will both have seen the new Bond film when we get to meet up.

Hope you have a good half-term holiday, too. We have grandchildren staying and may take them to Dalkeith Country Park to play on the Fort out there - it's great fun!

Thank you for writing, Max.

Best wishes,

Sheila

Hi Selina,

Thanks for writing! That's so cool that your favourite subject is art and that you love to draw. Drawing and painting are some of my favourite things to do as well. Alongside English and maths, I tutor people online in art & design. A couple of my youngest students even live in Malaysia! So teaching art online can be pretty awesome.

It's really interesting that you're keen to learn how to animate. I taught myself how to create stop-motion and hand-drawn animations when I was a teenager, and loved it! You should check out Muybridge's photos of animals moving. A lot of animators still use them as references. The first thing I ever practiced animating was Muybridge's flying bird: I printed out the photos, traced them and added colour, took photos of my drawings and made a GIF with them (you can also skim through the photos on a phone). That was when I saw that I had brought something to life! It takes a lot of time and patience but it's worth it. Let me know how you get on with animating once you get started. If you created an anime, what would the story be?

What is it like having lived in both China and Scotland? I can just imagine how tasty your mum's food is! I think my favourite Chinese dish is duck pancakes with hoisin sauce. I haven't tried hotpot yet, but I've heard it's delicious! I've lived in Scotland pretty much my whole life, but my parents lived in the Middle East for 10 years, and my mum still likes to cook and

# Selina & Lauren

*Letter 1 - Selina to Lauren*

I draw doodles for fun.

I like to swim and skip.

I like watching anime. I've watched *HxH KNY* and I've never finished *AOT* and I'm starting *JOJO*.

My favourite food is hot pot because I like eating spicy food.

My favourite subject is art because I really enjoy drawing. I really want to learn to animate and my parents bought me a board to animate but it has not arrived yet.

I'm half Chinese. My mum is Chinese and I lived in China until the age of five. My mum makes amazing Chinese food.

If I could go somewhere, I would go to Greece just to relax and eat a lot of food.

*Letter 2 - Lauren to Selina*

Hi Selina,

Thanks for writing! That's so cool that your favourite subject is art and that you love to draw. Drawing and painting are some of my favourite things to do as well. Alongside English and maths, I tutor people online in art and design. A couple of my youngest students even live in

Malaysia! So teaching art online can be pretty awesome.

It's really interesting that you're keen to learn how to animate. I taught myself to create stop-motion and hand-drawn animations when I was a teenager and loved it! You should check out Muybridge's photos of animals moving. A lot of animators still use them as references. The first thing I ever practiced animating was Muybridge's flying bird. I printed out the photos, traced them and added colour, took photos of my drawings and made a GIF with them (you can also skim through the photos on a phone). That was when I saw that I had brought something to life! It takes a lot of time and patience but it's worth it. Let me know how you get on with animating once you get started. If you created an anime, what would the story be?

What is it like having lived in both China and Scotland? I can just imagine how tasty your mum's food is! I think my favourite Chinese dish is duck pancakes with hoisin sauce. I haven't tried hotpot yet, but I've heard it's delicious!

I've lived in Scotland pretty much my whole life, but my parents lived in the Middle East for 10 years, and my mum still likes to cook and eat the food that they had over there, which I love as well!

Greece is a great choice of place to visit, and I think you're right: they have big, amazing family dinners there. I think I'd choose to visit Italy. There are art galleries and museums on every corner in the cities, and I know their pizza and pasta would be way better than what we have here. Food tourism all the way! Where else would you visit if you got the chance to go anywhere you liked?

I look forward to reading your next letter soon. Have a great weekend when it comes.

Best wishes,

Lauren

(P.S. Feel free to doodle on your letters to me if you like!)

*Letter 3 - Selina to Lauren*

Dear Lauren,

Thanks for your letter. Your handwriting is beautiful. This is my first time writing a letter to someone, so it might be a bit weird. I really like Maths and English, too. Many people think it's boring but learning a new formula or finding a new way to solve a new question is really exciting.

I really like reading books. I really like fantasy stories and I'm a big Harry Potter fan. I also like Greek and Roman mythology. I've been to Greece already, but I was in a hurry so I didn't get to relax that much. I will visit Italy someday. My name is the same as the Roman goddess of the Moon (Greek version is Selene). My favourite Greek monster is the Chimera. I've always wanted one as a pet.

Life in China is busy. We have a lot of homework and exams and the teachers use our break time to finish their classes. But we have some really fun activities like camping. My favourite activity was the day the school became a mini city and we spent half of our time running our own shop and half our time shopping. I haven't really been to that many places in China because when it's holiday time, everyone goes out and there's a lot of traffic jams and it's hard to book a ticket.

I haven't got my graphic tablet yet because my mum decided to buy it from China (because it's cheaper). One of my family friends, who wants to go to university in London, will bring it with her so I'll only get my tablet at the end of October. But I had an idea of a character.

I always wanted to draw a character of my own, but most of the time I draw cat girls, so I had an idea of a silver fox. I had an idea that my character can see people's thoughts and what they want to become, and she needs a piece of paper to stop her from seeing these things so that she can communicate with people normally. I hope you like her and reply soon.

Best wishes, Selina
(P.S. There might be a few spelling mistakes.)

*Letter 4 - Lauren to Selina*

Hi Selina,

Thanks for your letter, and your drawings, too. I love your character sketches: a chimera would definitely be a cool pet, especially if it was a three-headed cat! Silver-fox girl looks like an interesting character, and I'm super intrigued by the story idea. Does the paper absorb people's thoughts like water and turn them into written words? Maybe by the end of a single day, she's carrying a whole heavy book of pages, and her room is getting fuller and fuller of these books of people's thoughts and ambitions, but her parents just think they're books from the library?

I studied creative writing at university, so I love reading and writing, too. Do you have a favourite book or books? It's hard for me to choose mine, but one of my top three is *Gone with the Wind*. It's set during the American Civil War in the 1860s and follows a 16-year-old girl called Scarlett as she tries to survive. I love that Scarlett is actually horrible - she's selfish, sneaky, and spoilt. But you still admire her strength and she becomes a better person through the novel. Historical fiction is my favourite book genre. I also love historical films and TV shows. When I was your age, I loved *His Dark Materials*, *The City of Ember* and *The Hunger Games*.

I like the idea of pretending that school is a mini city. Then you can get to experience what it's like balancing work and leisure like an adult. Did you get pretend money to use as well? What kind of shops were there for you to work at? Did you get to choose?

I know exactly what you mean about feeling excited and proud when you suddenly 'get' a new method or formula in maths. I didn't used to like maths much at school, but now that I tutor it, I like it a lot. They say teaching someone something is the best way to learn it properly yourself, because you have to have the confidence to share your own knowledge. Do you have an idea yet of what you'd like to study when you're a bit older or what career you'd like?

I've not been to Greece or Italy yet, but I did get to study abroad in Copenhagen (the capital city of Denmark) a few years ago and loved it. The weather is pretty much like Scotland. They have amazing pastries and beautiful lakes. Most people speak English there, but they also speak Danish, which sounds very strange at first - a bit like there's something stuck at the back of people's throats! I like learning songs in different languages and know a couple in Danish (my favourite is 'Øde Ø' (pronounced ood-ih oo), which means 'Desert Island'). I know one song in Chinese from a friend, too.

Looking forward to reading your next letter!

Best wishes,

Lauren

---

*Letter 5 - Selina to Lauren*

Dear Lauren,

Thanks for your letter. I've never thought about the paper attached to her hood. I think the paper acts like a shield that stops her from seeing people's thoughts, but your idea is much cooler.

I don't have a favourite book. It's so hard to choose. Now I'm reading a book called *The Crow Boy*. It's about a boy called Tom that moved from Manchester to Edinburgh. On a school trip to Mary King's Close, he follows this girl called Annie, then goes back in time to 1645 of the Edinburgh plague. I started this book because the first words were 'Tom hates Edinburgh'. My city isn't the coolest city on earth but still you can't hate it.

There's another book called *Being Chinglish* (I think, I can't remember). When I first read the title I was so excited. Like I don't know if I'm more Chinese or British. So I'll start that book after I've finished *Crow Boy*. (Also, I'm obsessed with crows and crow face masks. I wanted to dress up as a crow doctor during Halloween but there were no right sizes for me.)

I haven't really read that many historical books. I had an amazing set of books about the history of China and I loved it. Sadly, I've left my books in China. In fact, I've left most cool stuff in China. Now I'm sitting at home reading *Horrible History*, laughing at the terrible jokes and trying not to be sick at some of the facts. I've got the *Horrible History* version of the history of Edinburgh and Scotland. I've read the one on Edinburgh. Oh boy, it was bloody. At least it's not as bad as the history of China. I really feel a bit sorry for my mates in China to learn 5,000 years of history and doing a lot of homework.

Best wishes,

Selina

---

*Letter 6 - Lauren to Selina*

Dear Selina,

I see what you mean about your character's hood now. That's a really interesting idea to explore in a story: being able to read people's minds. Like so many people would love to, but actually not wanting to have that special power because maybe it's too overwhelming. You should definitely keep working on it!

*The Crow Boy* sounds like a book I would enjoy! I love stories about travelling back in time, and I'm also really interested in the history of Edinburgh in particular. Like you say, it can get quite gruesome, but it's so special finding out what life was like for ordinary people in this exact same place hundreds of years ago. I started developing a story idea inspired by the miniature coffins that were found on Arthur's Seat 200 years ago. You can actually see them in the National Museum of Scotland. There were 77 of them in total, all about the length of your palm, and they're a total mystery – no one knows why they were made. But after analysing the materials they're made of, it was discovered that they were probably made by a shoemaker. So I've used that as inspiration for a novel.

*Horrible Histories* is great! I didn't watch much of it when I was younger, actually I've probably seen more as an adult! I like the film they made about Shakespeare called *Bill*, and I've still got the rap stuck in my head that Henry VIII does about his wives.

Crows are very interesting birds. They're extremely smart! Apparently, they can recognise human faces and remember people for up to five years. I even read a story that a little girl made friends with a crow that came to her garden, and it gave her gifts like buttons and hair clasps in return for the food she left.

The plague masks are super creepy. You could totally make your own one. That would be a great Halloween costume! Maybe your character creates her own paper plague mask as well, so that she can still go out trick-or-treating with a paper shield.

I don't know much about Chinese history, which is a shame really. You never really get taught about it in schools here – only British history, especially battles and such, on the whole. I suppose you can't cover the history of every country on the planet in weekly history lessons, but the history of China is so rich and ancient (5,000 years is certainly a long time!), it would be good to know more about it. The Terracotta Warriors are incredible.

Hope you have a great weekend!

Best wishes,

Lauren

---

*Letter 7 - Selina to Lauren*

Dear Lauren,

Thanks for the letter. I've just had two exams this week and I've got two A's. Yeah :) I have a test next Monday, so I hope I get an A or an A+.

Today, 1st October, is National Day of China, so I think I'm going to talk about it here. China has 5,000 years of history, but actually, if you count from when characters were invented, it's 3,700 years.

At first China was a bunch of tribes and their 'elected' leader, until one man called Yu (he is a hero because he dealt with flooding at that time and saved a lot of lives) decided to give his town to his son. So the first dynasty was born: Xia Dynasty. Xia lasted for quite a long time (I can't remember how long), until there was this horrible king that thought he was as great as the sun.

At that time, people groaned at the sun. They said, 'Oh, why wouldn't you die, sun?' to express their hatred to the King. He spent a lot of money on a very fancy palace with a big pool of wine and meat hanging. He and his many wives played in the pool and ate the meat when they were hungry, while people were starving. So he had to go. A little tribe took over and the second dynasty was born: Shang.

Shang has a very interesting name. Shang literally means business. I'm not sure why they always have weird names. Shang did not learn its lesson from previous dynasties. It had the most terrifying tyrant ever (Zhou). Legend says he was so strong that he could catch two bulls with his bare hands. He was a wise king at the start, but one lady changes the whole story: Daji.

Legend says that she is a spirit/nine-tailed fox (a fox that can shapeshift into humans and do magic; my character is a nine-tailed fox, too). She was sent by an ancient Chinese goddess to end the dynasty.

So it had to go. The next dynasty, Zhou Dynasty – also my Chinese surname – was a messy one. Six little kingdoms fought each other until one man, Qing Shi Huang (literally means the First Empire), made China one country for the first time, and everyone used the same language. Yeah! But this great dynasty did not last long, because the second emperor was a puppet.

So it had to go. Then the Han Dynasty, the greatest dynasty along with the Tang Dynasty. At that time, China was like the biggest bully in Asia. Other countries were honoured to trade with it, including the Roman

Empire, along the Silk Road. But all good times have to end. The empire was split into three kingdoms and over the next hundreds of years, China was fighting each other. So that's the first half of the history of China. I hope you like it.

Best Wishes,

Selina

(P.S.: Can you teach me how to write in a fancy way?)

---

*Letter 8 - Lauren to Selina*

Hi Selina,

Congratulations on your brilliant test results! You must be working super hard. Keep it up!

Thank you for your crash course in Chinese history. Reading it was like watching a really exciting trailer for a film, haha! I'll definitely look more into it. Mythology is such an interesting part of history as well, like the nine-tailed fox, and how animals represent different things in various cultures. I think my favourite mythological creature is the Selkie. It's from Scottish folklore and is a creature that can shapeshift from a seal in the ocean into a woman on land.

I taught myself to write 'r's' this fancy way a few years ago, a bit like Jane Austen (I used to write them like 'r'). I've been practicing calligraphy using a quill pen recently. It can be tricky and technical, but it's also creative and quite relaxing once you get the hang of it. Some of the videos online of people doing calligraphy are mesmerising!

It's been so nice writing to you and receiving your letters over the past few weeks. I'll miss reading them! Hopefully we'll be able to meet in person sometime soon. Until then.

Best wishes,

Lauren

# Shaun & Liz

*Letter 1 - Shaun to Liz*

Dear Liz,

Hello. My name is Shaun. I like video games, writing and reading.

I live in Scotland. My favourite food is sushi, my favourite game is *Terraria*. I have two cats and two dogs.

Recently in school I have been learning how to count to 1,000 in Mandarin.

What is your favourite food? What is your favourite animal? Do you play video games too? Do you have any pets? And if so, what are their names? Do you read books? If so, what is your favourite genre?

Have a good day/evening.

Shaun

*Letter 2 - Liz to Shaun*

Dear Shaun,

I was very pleased to receive your letter, written so well and full of interesting facts about your interests. I hope mine will be as good.

I have a son who also likes video games. He plays *FIFA* a lot with his friends. I sometimes think he plays it too much, but I am an older generation and didn't grow up playing computer games. He does also play a lot of sport, so I don't really mind as long as there is a balance.

I am very impressed that you like sushi. You have very good taste, as I also like sushi. I like California rolls. My daughter, who is a doctor, makes very good sushi. You have to soak the rice in water with vinegar to make it sticky, then you have to have a special mat to roll them up. I think it's easier to buy it. I like cooking and my favourite food is steak and chips, which I have every Friday. I am a creature of habit. I like inviting friends for dinner and always lay the table with my best crockery and glasses and have lots of candles and flowers. I put candles all around the house to make it look cosy.

You are full of surprises. Learning to count in Mandarin will not be easy. I have visited China a few times and like it there very much. I have been to Xian, where the Terracotta Warriors are, and I have been to Beijing and walked along the Great Wall of China. It is an amazing experience.

I am envious that you have two cats and two dogs. I would love to have a dog, but I work every day and it would not be fair to leave it at home alone for so long. My daughter has two cats and I occasionally look after them if she goes away. They are Maine Coons called Nix and Lireal. They can take time to become affectionate, but I bribe them with chicken breast, which they love. They are indoor cats and I always think it is a bit sad that they can't enjoy the fresh air. Nix sits in the window and looks out at the garden a lot. I did once take them outside on leads, but they did not like it at all, so I think they are happy to be inside in the warm.

I also like reading. I read all kinds of books from biographies to classic literature. I have read a lot of John Grisham. He writes about American law cases where ordinary people are being intimidated by Big Industry. Usually the ordinary people win, which is good, but that's not always the case in reality. Fiction is a good way to create the ending you want.

I think you must have a very good imagination. Always value your imagination and continue to read. Reading gives us lots to think about and helps us see different views.

There was a music and arts festival near my house over the weekend. It was quite noisy until late. But it was good to see people getting together and enjoying themselves. I like listening to music and recently my son bought some vinyls and a record player. It's fun to sit in the evening listening to records. We go to markets to collect new records. His grandfather gave him some very old ones from the 1920s and 1950s. Do you like music? What is your favourite kind and who are the bands/artists you listen to? I have all my music on my phone and still buy from the Apple Store, but most people now use Spotify. I will need to catch up on the technology.

I look forward to receiving your reply. It can be hard thinking of interesting things to write about, but just tell me the things you normally do with your friends or at school. Everyday life is full of interesting things. Sharing thoughts and ideas is really valuable. It's good to understand how we are all different.

I look forward to discovering more about you.

Best wishes, Liz

---

*Letter 3 - Shaun to Liz*

Dear Liz,

To answer your question, I enjoy music. My favourite genres are indie pop and British rap. I mostly listen to girl in red, Digga D, and Central Cee.

My brother has cats and they are also indoor cats. I thought it was sad at first, but I realised sometimes it's better, as many cats can feel a lot more stress when going out versus staying inside.

I would love to get a chance to go to China, as it seems a beautiful and a historically rich place to visit.

Recently one of my dogs has been very sick and has something wrong with her eye. I find it extremely sad as she has been in my life for nine to 10 years. She will be going for a test next week. I'll keep you updated.

Have a great day.

Shaun

---

*Letter 4 - Liz to Shaun*

Dear Shaun,

Thank you for your lovely reply. So nice to hear from you.

Firstly, I want to say I'm very sorry that your dog is poorly. That is a shame and hopefully everything will be well after the test, or there will be a treatment that will make her better. Our pets are really like members of the family, so it causes a lot of worry when they are not 100%. I hope you are OK.

I was very interested to hear your choice of music. Being a dinosaur, I have not heard of any of those artists, but I will try to YouTube them over the weekend so I get a flavour of the genre. My son and I were at a local market at Brunswick Street on Sunday and we bought a vinyl – Dire Straits, *Moving Pictures*. Have you heard of them? I like wandering around the market and there are some nice antique stalls that I enjoy browsing. I like collecting Willow china, so am always on the lookout for some new pieces. There is also a fantastic bakery nearby that sells the best ever almond croissants. So I indulged myself.

I am up very early this morning as I have a very busy day. I am chairing a Green Tourism event, speaking on a panel about data and attending a board meeting, then rushing off to a fancy dinner at the Botanic Gardens. I have a lot to prepare. It's funny sitting at the kitchen table with it still dark outside. We are now very much into autumn! I don't particularly like getting up early, but sometimes we have to just get on with it. I am looking forward to the weekend.

I will be going to Glasgow to see my daughter on Saturday. It is her birthday, so we will have a nice walk in the park and a coffee while I give her presents. She is going out with her friends in the evening, so I will have a nice quiet evening at home, back in Edinburgh. Do you go out with your friends? What things do you do on weekends?

I will need to go now to write my presentations and read up on data! What a fun day!

I look forward to our next exchange of correspondence.

Very best wishes

Liz

---

*Letter 5 - Shaun to Liz*

Dear Liz,

I have heard about Dire Straits, although I've never actually listened to them. And to answer your other two questions: I go out with my friends every now and then and on the weekends I tend to go to my brother's to help him with things.

You're right that autumn is in full swing as the mornings keep on getting colder and wetter. I have been wanting to go to the market, but never had time to. If I'm lucky I may be able to go this weekend, but it isn't likely, because I have a decent bit of homework to catch up on. Happy birthday to your daughter. I hope she has a good day, and it isn't ruined by the rain. It's a shame that's a lot to ask for, given the time of year.

It's sad this is the last letter I will send.

Have a great day,

Shaun

*Letter 6 - Liz to Shaun*

Dear Shaun,

It is indeed sad that these are our last letters to each other. I have enjoyed our correspondence. Sounds like you are a very good brother and nice that you see your brother often and help him out.

I don't know where the time passes. Here we are in October and I imagine Christmas will arrive in no time. I am planning a few days off in a few weeks. My son will be on half term, so it will be nice to spend some time together. We live quite near the Firth of Forth and like to walk along the shore. Being near the sea always makes me feel happy. One of my favourite things to do is walk along a beach looking for shells and heart-shaped stones. I have lots of jars full of the shells I have collected.

I am also planning a trip to Wales. My family lives there and I visit a few times a year. I grew up in Wales but came to Edinburgh to study and fell in love with Scotland, so never went back home. I have been here a very long time and feel more Scottish than Welsh now, except when there is a rugby match, Scotland versus Wales! It takes about seven hours to drive to Wales, but I quite like driving and I like to listen to the radio. I'm not keen on getting stuck in traffic jams on the motorway, which happens from time to time. The longest journey took 12 hours – not much fun.

I hope that you will continue writing. You have a lovely manner and maybe should think of writing a diary or entering short story competitions. I think you could do very well.

I believe there are plans for us all to meet up towards the end of the year, when things become a bit more normal. I very much look forward to meeting you. It has been such a pleasure getting to know you a bit.

Work hard and take care and thank you for your lovely and interesting letters.

Best wishes,

Liz

# Tor & Lucy

*Letter 1 - Tor to Lucy*

I like to play sports or watch TV or play on my PS4.

My favourite sports are basketball and badminton.

My favourite show is *Brooklyn Nine-Nine*, but I also like *The Flash*.

My favourite food is beef burgers.

My favourite subject is H.F.T because I like food. :)

I would like to go to Australia.

*Letter 2 - Lucy to Tor*

Dear Tor,

Thanks for your letter which I enjoyed reading. It's good to meet you! I'll tell you a bit about me and I'd love to hear more about you next time you write.

I live in Leith with my husband and two boys aged 14 and 10 (well, almost 11) – they're all mad about football so watching and playing football are the main activities in our house. My younger son also likes watching *Brooklyn Nine-Nine*, it's very funny – I think he's seen every episode.

You mentioned you like sport, do you like football too?

And who do you live with at home?

Do you have any pets?

We have a white fluffy cat called Star. He came from the cat rescue home so he's quite shy. We call him a 'feardy cat' but he's very lovely and affectionate too. He usually sleeps in one of the kid's beds at night.

I work as a graphic designer – at the moment I'm designing Scotland's COVID Memorial which I can tell you more about if you're interested. It's being designed to remember people's experiences of the pandemic.

How did you find homeschool? Did you prefer it to being at school with your friends? I found it very hard being stuck at home all the time for months on end.

Tell me more about H.F.T. and what you like to cook. My favourite food is Italian but I'm not a very good cook so I love eating out! And best of all I love going to Italy – Rome is my favourite city in the world.

Hope to hear back from you soon.

From Lucy

---

*Letter 3 - Tor to Lucy*

Dear Lucy,

Thank you for your letter. It was really interesting. It was nice to learn about you!

I live in Stockbridge with my brother, who's seven years old, and my mum and dad.

I do not like football that much but I really like basketball, badminton and swimming.

I currently do not have any pets, but I really want a dog. (A Husky in particular.)

What is your favourite TV show?

What is your favourite movie?

What is your dream job?

My favourite thing I've cooked is pizza, which is one of my favourite foods!

Hope to hear from you soon!

From Tor

---

*Letter 4 - Lucy to Tor*

Dear Tor,

Thanks for your letter. It's funny to hear you live in Stockbridge, because I grew up there with my mum and dad, two sisters, and a brother. We had a dog (a Spaniel) called Sheena, so I remember taking her for walks to Inverleith Park. We used to watch the remote control boats on the pond there and our dog used to chase the ducks.

You asked about my favourite TV show. Well, that's probably *Doc Martin*. It's very funny, and also we go to Cornwall on holiday every summer, so I like recognising the places that are familiar in the show.

My favourite movies are very varied, from James Bond (can't wait for the new release next week) to *Shrek* and other funny kids movies. I watch a lot of films with our kids. Did you see *Free Guy*?

My dream job would be to be a successful novel writer. I would love to use my imagination to write and craft a perfect story that people of all ages would get enjoyment from reading – like J.K. Rowling or Roald Dahl.

I like eating pizza, too, and Italy is my favourite country, so that's what I love to eat when I go there! In Edinburgh, my favourite pizzeria is Origano on Leith Walk.

Tell me more about what you like to do. Do you go away anywhere nice on holiday with your family?

Hope to hear back from you again soon.

Lucy

---

**Letter 5 - Tor to Lucy**

Dear Lucy,

Thanks for your letter, Lucy. I really enjoyed reading it. I also like *Doc Martin*, but my all-time favourite show has to be *Brooklyn Nine-Nine*. I'm also very excited for the new James Bond release coming out!

Yes, I have seen *Free Guy* and I loved it. It was so unexpectedly funny in awkward situations.

You mentioned liking J.K. Rowling and Roald Dahl. Are they your favourite authors? My favourite authors are Chris Bradford, Jeff Kinney and my top favourite is Anthony Horotwitz.

I like eating pizza, too, and my favourite place to have it in a restaurant is Pizza Express and my favourite place to order from is Papa John's.

And, finally, you asked me if there was anywhere I liked to go on holiday. I really like going to Spain, but I absolutely love going to Florida.

From, Tor

---

**Letter 6 - Lucy to Tor**

Hi, Tor.

Great to hear back from you. We have some things in common! We like the same food, books and movies. I'm not sure how old you are, but my sons are 14 and almost 11, so I guess I enjoy a lot of the things that they enjoy.

It sounds like you read a lot of books. That's fantastic because it's such a special thing to do when you have time. It helps you grow your imagination and I find reading is like an adventure into another world. I've never been successful at encouraging my older son to read, so if you have any tips that might work for him, please let me know! My younger son loves Jeff Kinney, too. We quite often read his books together.

You're lucky to have been to Florida. It's an exciting place isn't it? Quite different to Edinburgh, anyway. I went a long time ago and went on a hovercraft across the Everglades and saw turtles and alligators. You don't see many of those in the Water of Leith!

Hope you have a good weekend. We have tickets to see *No Time To Die*. Hurray, it's here at last!!

Have fun whatever you get up to,

From, Lucy

---

*Letter 7 - Tor to Lucy*

Hi Lucy,

Good to hear back from you. You're right, we do have a lot in common! If your older son likes James Bond (speaking of which, I'm watching tonight!), he might like *Alex Rider* and *Bodyguard*.

I really like them because they are both quite similar, and they are about teenagers as spies and bodyguards. Also, I really think he would enjoy them.

Yes, it's very lucky that I got to Florida. I went jet skiing and went to the beach many times. It was amazing!

I hope you enjoy the movie.

From,

Tor

*Letter 8 - Lucy to Tor*

Hi, Tor.

Thanks so much for your letter and for the reading suggestions. We watched the *Alex Rider* movie and that was great, as you say very like James Bond! I'll recommend that to my son.

We saw *No Time to Die* at the weekend and I think it was my favourite all time 007 movie, except I really didn't like the way it ended – it was so sad. I won't spoil it for you in case you haven't seen it yet!

I hope things are going well for you at school. The most important thing is to find something you really enjoy doing and that way you're likely to be good at it. And you'll enjoy learning at school!

My main thing at school was art and design, and I've been running a creative business for the past 17 years, so I've realised that the things I worried about at school (like not being at all good at chemistry) really don't matter now.

Find something you love to do and enjoy doing your best at it!

Wishing you all the very best whatever you do. I've really enjoyed being your pen pal.

Lucy

Growing up in the mountains, I saw mostly black bears, elk, and mountain goats. Oh, and lots of deer. When I was older I got to see beavers, moose, and lots of buffalo. Someday I hope to see

15/09/2021

Dear Tristan,

I'm so excited to have a pen pal! I've written to friends and family before, but never to an official pen pal. Have you?

It's cool that you want to be a vet someday. Science was always hard for me. Do you have a favourite animal? (I really love cows.) I have a dog named Django. He's a Norwegian Elkhound and my best pal.

I was really happy to read that you want to see North America and Africa! My sister has been to Africa but I haven't. I've been to North America because that's where I'm from! Which parts do you want to see?

# Tristan & Charlotte

*Letter 1 - Tristan to Charlotte*

I play Yu-Gi-Oh!, an anime card-trading game, with my brother for fun. I also play *Minecraft* and watch YouTube.

I don't really like sport, but I play cricket and hockey.

I don't watch much TV, but I like watching Marvel and *Doctor Who* and I like various other movies.

My favourite food is salty fries. I am a pescatarian, except when I go to a restaurant, where I have meat.

I like science and I would like to be a vet when I am older. I also find science interesting.

I have two brothers; I am the middle child. I have a mum and a dad, my mum has a health company and my dad is a director and editor. I also have two white cats.

I would like to travel to North America if given the chance. But I would like to go to Africa to see the wildlife.

I am good at drawing and have an eye for photography. I used to be good at chess and one of my cats is deaf.

*Letter 2 - Charlotte to Tristan*

Dear Tristan,

I'm so excited to have a pen pal! I've written to friends and family before, but never to an official pen pal. Have you?

It's cool that you want to be a vet someday. Science was always hard for me. Do you have a favourite animal? (I really love cows.) I have a dog named Django. He's a Norwegian Elkhound and my best pal.

I was really happy to read that you want to see North America and Africa! My sister has been to Africa but I haven't. I've been to North America because that's where I'm from! Which parts do you want to see? Growing up in the mountains, I saw mostly bears, elk and mountain goats. Oh, and lots of deer. When I was older, I got to see beavers, moose and lots of buffalo. Someday I hope to see a whale and a polar bear.

I can't wait to read your letter. What's your favourite Marvel movie? Do both of your brothers like Yu-Gi-Oh? What do you like to draw?

Your new friend,

Charlotte

*Letter 3 - Tristan to Charlotte*

Dear Charlotte,

I am glad you are happy to have me as a pen pal.

I would have loved to grow up in the mountains next to lots of wildlife.

Where in North America did you grow up? In Alaska, America, or Canada?

This is the first time I have had a pen pal.

I have stayed in the area I was born in for most of my life, but when a holiday comes my family and I travel a bit.

I am usually way better at drawing than this drawing of me.

I like drawing animals and fantasy creatures.

My favourite Marvel movie is probably *Spider-Man: Homecoming*. Both my brothers like Yu-Gi-Oh!, but my little brother plays it more with me.

My questions:

What are your hobbies? What do you like to do?

How old are you? And if you have one, what is your job? Not trying to be rude.

Where do you live now and how old is Django – in human years?

Can't wait for your next letter.

Tristan

---

*Letter 4 - Charlotte to Tristan*

Dear Tristan,

Silly me! In my excitement I forgot to tell you much about myself.

I'm from western Canada. My first home was a tiny town in British Columbia. It was close to the US border and nestled in the mountains, so we skied a lot. When I was nine I moved to Alberta, to a town in the Rocky Mountains. After high school, I moved to the capital city, Edmonton, for several years.

Now I'm 28 (my birthday was exactly one month ago today!) and I've lived in Edinburgh for two years. I love living in Leith because I can walk or bike pretty much everywhere I need to go.

I just graduated university with a Master's degree and hope to find a good job soon. I work part-time at the Commonwealth Pool, but it's not what I want to do. I want to work with young writers.

I love your drawings! Especially the expression on the cat's face. Here's me and Django:

*Likes:*
- swimming
- reading
- nature

*Dislikes:*
- super hot weather
- cucumbers

He turned 6 in July... so I guess that's 42 in human years. Or is it the other way around?

I'll have to watch *Spider-Man: Homecoming*. *Into the Spider-Verse* was great. I still love the old Spider-Man movies with Tobey Maguire.

How come you decided to be a pescatarian? (I'm a vegetarian and my mum and sister are pescatarians!) I did it on a dare when I was 13 and just never stopped!

Are you excited that autumn is here? Do you like school? What year are you in? (Am I asking that right? In Canada we say grade.)

Charlotte

---

*Letter 5 - Tristan to Charlotte*

Hello Charlotte,

It's OK you didn't say much about yourself. I got a bit excited, as well. So I guess you did lots of moving when you were younger. I only moved once when I was about two years old, but somehow I still remember it. I sometimes can remember a memory from years ago, but not what I had for breakfast. What did I have for breakfast?

Anyway, congrats on graduating with a Master's degree! I don't know much about university, but I assume that's a good degree. And good luck on finding a job you enjoy! I like your drawings and I'm glad you like mine. And I agree, too: hot weather is not good. I have seen *Spider-Verse* as well, and it is still one of my favourite films.

The reason I became pescatarian is because I don't think a species should be harvested for another's enjoyment.

I'm 13 years old and am in S2/year two. I like most school subjects, but some not so much. Apparently this will be the last letter I will write to you.

What is your favourite movie? I don't really have any other questions, so if you want, just tell me a bit more about you. Thanks for being my pen pal.

From, Tristan

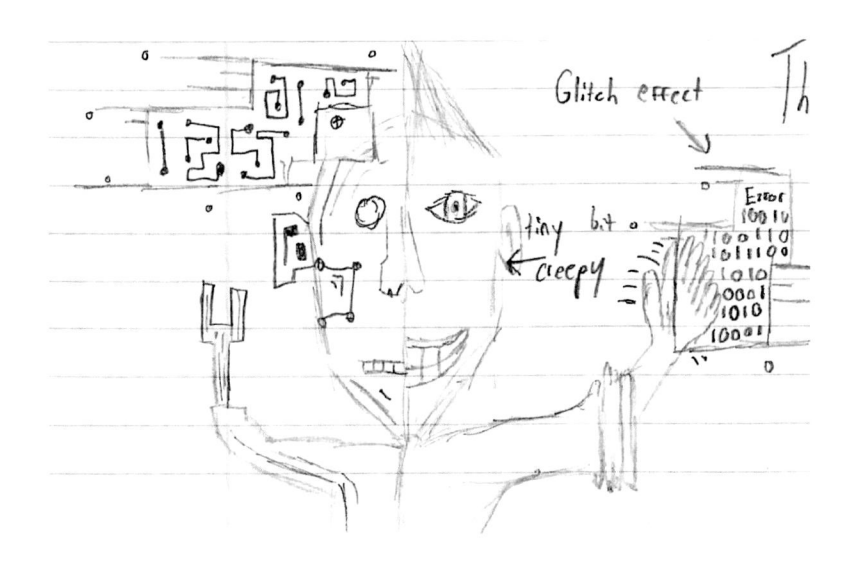

*Letter 6 - Charlotte to Tristan*

Dear Tristan,

Thank you for sending me another drawing in your last letter. October is the perfect time for tiny bit creepy things, don't you think? I'll have to practice that flitch effect! I'm not as good at robotic/techy stuff. Do you get into the spirit of spookiness in the autumn?

My partner and I watch lots of scary or creepy movies - anything Halloween-ish. Tonight I made pumpkin soup for dinner and walked Django through the turning leaves. Autumn comes much earlier back home. It's all yellow and orange there.

I am a huge *Scooby Doo* fan. (Dogs? Mysteries? A groovy van? Count me in!!!) But so far I haven't found a good way to watch it. That will be my mission this month.

I agree that animals deserve to live for reasons other than human enjoyment. I don't mind when other people eat meat, but I can't do it. It's been 15 years since I last ate meat! When I went vegetarian I was the same age you are now.

My favourite movie changes a lot. I do love the *Guernsey Literary and Potato Peel Pie Society*, though the book was better. And I never get tired of *Mamma Mia!* Though I probably like the live stage show more. I've seen it live four times! I think I like movies that make me happy and TV shows that are more sad.

I've really enjoyed being your pen pal. It's nice to learn about someone in my new country. I wish you all the best with the school year! Thanks for the encouragement about the job. :)

Your pal,

Charlotte

# ACKNOWLEDGEMENTS

A huge thank you to Broughton High School Headteacher John Wilson, Head of English Nicola Daniel, and teachers Rory Brown and Tammi Anderson for continuing to welcome us into your school's community. Every Friday, Mr Brown and Ms Anderson greeted the SPA team into their classrooms, allowing us to take over their classes and work with their pupils. Each day was a challenge and a joy, and we are grateful for the opportunity to help create this book. Thank you for all that you did for us and do for your pupils!

Thank you to Jessica Armstrong who as workshop leader helped to engage and encourage the pupils to take letter writing seriously and welcome the joy it can bring. Thanks to Alisa Lindsay who designed the layout of this book (www.alisalindsay.myportfolio.com) and to Jonathan Gould who designed the covers.

This book was created and published with the support of the J.P. Marland Charitable Trust. The biggest of thanks to our letter writers, the wonderful pupils of Broughton High School and our dedicated volunteers! Your openness, honesty, and hard work were truly a joy to behold. Thank you for trusting us with your letters!

## VOLUNTEERS

The volunteers of the Super Power Agency are integral to our projects. Our in-school programmes could not happen without their ideas, drive and kindness. They help unleash our young people's most important super power: creativity!

We would like to extend the warmest of thanks to every volunteer who joined us on this project:

## PEN PALS

| | | |
|---|---|---|
| Megan Rudden | Mary Siggs | Lesley McMillian |
| Lucy Gray | Adrian Mead | Eileen Shand |
| Valerie Lindsay | Dave Rogers | Sian Bevan |
| Nick Reid | Sarah Gibson | Elaine Moran |
| Lavina Rodger | Susan Nickalls | Amerdeep Dhami |
| Eilidh Cameron | Liz Mcareavey | Stephanie Mlot |
| Charlotte Cranston | Angela Blacklock-Brown | Linsey Shields |
| Lauren Ross | | Janice McNeillie |
| Eduardo Rodriguez | Johanna Barre | Francis Lake |
| Olivia Brunton | Emma Struthers | Steph Patmore |
| Lucy Doherty | Jo Schaab | Claire Sawers |
| Johnny Brown | Claire Heffernan | Vlada Nebo |
| Sheila Yarrow | Catherine Lindow | Ryan Lawrie |
| Maxine Sloss | Fiona Lowe | Martin Dewar |
| Alastair Chisholm | Will Blair | |

## E.L.E.P.H.A.N.T

*The Extraordinary League of Editors, Proofreaders, Helpers & Nifty Typists:*

**Typists**
Monica Kassouf
David Robinson
Emma Struthers
Celise Downs
Will Blair
Jo Schaab

**Editors**
Fiona Lowe
Craig Mckercher
Stephanie Mlot
David Creighton-Offord
Monica Kassouf
Paula Campbell
Ailsa Purdie
Gav Inglis
Janice McNellie
Helen Bleck
David Robinson

SUPER POWER AGENCY
Registered Charity SC046550

STAFF
Gerald Richards, Founding CEO
Claire Heffernan, Volunteer Coordinator
Linsey Shields, Fundraising and Development Manager
Leia Sherman, Social Media Coordinator

TRUSTEES
Valerie Lindsay, Chair
Maxine Sloss, Founder
Amerdeep Dhami
Ciara Gracie
Phoebe Grigor
Francis Lake
Ryan Lawrie
Elaine Moran
Ryan Van Winkle


FIND & FOLLOW
https://Superpoweragency.com
Instagram: @Superpoweragency
Facebook: @Superpoweragency
Twitter: @Superpow3
LinkedIn: @Superpoweragency